TIKAL

A HANDBOOK OF THE ANCIENT MAYA RUINS

With a Guide Map

WILLIAM R. COE

THE UNIVERSITY MUSEUM
UNIVERSITY OF PENNSYLVANIA
Philadelphia

CONTENTS

AN INTRODUCTION   5

THE VISITOR AT TIKAL   7

THE DISCOVERY OF TIKAL   12

THE RUINS   19

   Great Plaza   27

   Temple I   28

   Temple II   36

   Plaza and Terrace Monuments   37

   North Acropolis   41

   Great Plaza Ballcourt   50

   Pyramid with Perishable Temple   50

   Plaza Chultun   54

   Central Acropolis   55

   Palace Reservoir   71

   East Plaza   72

   West Plaza   74

   Temple III   76

   Bat Palace   77

   Twin-pyramid Complex N   77

   Tozzer Causeway   80

   Temple IV   80

   Maudslay Causeway   82

   Group H and Twin-pyramid Complex P   82

Twin-pyramid Complex M   82

Maler Causeway   84

Twin-pyramid Complexes Q, R, O   84

Twin-pyramid Complex L   87

Méndez Causeway   87

Temple of the Inscriptions   87

Plaza of the Seven Temples   88

Triple Ballcourt   90

Lost World Complex   90

South Acropolis   92

Temple V   92

Group F   93

Group G   93

THE CARVED MONUMENTS   94

THE GROWTH AND DECLINE OF TIKAL   98

APPENDIX: Maya Methods of Dating at Tikal   111

SELECTED BIBLIOGRAPHY   119

ACKNOWLEDGMENTS   127

THE AUTHOR   129

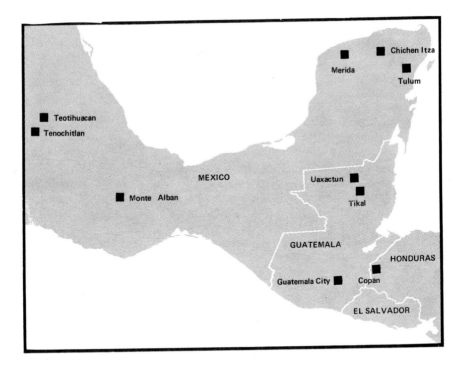

AN INTRODUCTION

Twenty-five hundred or more years ago a group of peoples settled on and about a low - lying hill in the lowland jungles of northern Guatemala. Their descendants were soon to create by almost unfathomable means one of the most astonishing civilizations the world has ever seen. We now know that hill and the surrounding area as Tikal. Tikal, a traditional name whose meaning is unknown to us, became the prime city of the Maya people populating the Peninsula of Yucatán. Today, in what is geographically the southern part of this peninsula, the pre-eminence of Tikal is still asserted by the ruined roof combs of huge white temples rising above an undulating rain forest that ends only at the distant Caribbean sea.

It is commonplace to speak of the splendid proud Maya, of their almost deified cities. Yet, such clichés are given renewed meaning —even superlatives, however florid, seem justified— when one stands in the midst of Tikal, or looks from a high temple doorway across the jungle that conquered the city and its Maya. We strive to understand Tikal, to rescue it for our edification by whatever means we have. It is old; it belongs to a people whose culture for the most part died long ago. It is separate, of other origins, without connections with the Old World. If its history and that of its makers have bearing on today, it lies most likely in the causes of civilization and those factors, both natural and human, that made it die. Tikal in an extreme way embodies the allure of the past and the archaeological dimension. Its muteness is assaulted by excavators who, after years of digging and studying, emerge from it all, from their potsherds and now-cleared buildings, to announce their facts and inferences. What they have to say (usually in heavy monographs) is really only a few significant words on what once was Tikal and the extraordinary people, with ancestors out of Asia 10,000 years ago, who lived in this now sparsely populated forest.

Since 1970 it has been possible to travel to Petén by car. To reach Tikal —a total distance of 554 kilometers— drive north out of Guatemala City on Highway CA-9 (Carretera del Atlántico) to the turn-off at Morales (Km. 244) to take the Morales to San Felipe branch, which reaches the bridge over the Río Dulce at Km. 274. This bridge at almost one kilometer in length is reputed to be the longest in Central America. After the crossing, the road goes through the towns of Modesto Méndez and Poptún before reaching Santa Elena and Flores and continuing around the eastern shore of Lake Petén Itzá to end at Tikal.

The visitors who come to Tikal are often people who have recently arrived from, or are scheduled soon to see, such other well known Mesoamerican sites as Copán, Palenque, Chichen Itzá, Tulum, Monte Alban, and Teotihuacán. They immediately wish to know where Tikal fits in time in relation to these other great Precolumbian centers.

The great eras of Copán and Palenque matched in time that of Tikal, while the florescent years of Chichen Itzá and Tulum, well to the north of Tikal, postdated its heyday. The great centuries of non-Maya Teotihuacán and Monte Alban, to the northwest of Tikal in Mexico, concurred and matched in time what we refer to as the Early Classic Period of Tikal (see p. 27), though all three sites had beginnings in the pre-Christian era.

There is no easy shortcut to history and less so in this part of the world where we have so few named kings and dates to which we may attach the momentous scraps of human existence that pass for history. To understand what went on, or may have gone on, in this part of ancient America the reader must read on beyond this simple guide. Every year people somewhere are poring over manuscripts, colonial histories, and the records of their excavations. Each year facts are added, speculations offered, and tentative conclusions reached and insights proffered, all to be sustained or beaten-down by the results of another decade of research. It is a fascinating, life-consuming process that always is committed to comprehending the causes and courses of civilization. As you wander about Tikal, we hope you are captivated by it as we are. Tikal —and beyond it— is a prodigious field that needs recruits.

View of Temple II from the doorway of Temple I. The roof combs of Temples III and IV can bee seen in the background.

THE VISITOR AT TIKAL

Fortunately for the visitor, the days of mule-back traveling to Tikal are over. By air 190 miles almost due north of Guatemala City, Tikal is served on a schedule by the excellent Guatemala airline, Aviateca, from whose office in Guatemala, or from any local or foreign tourist agency, reservations can be obtained. The flight north to Tikal first carries one over the mountainous, deep-valleyed area of highland Guatemala. This magnificent terrain shortly gives way as the mountains drop to the flat limestone base of the geographic Peninsula of Yucatán. First, the serpentine Rio de la Pasión, rimmed with ancient sites of the lowland Maya, can be sighted below on a clear day. Then gradually the heavy forest begins to break with the appearance of savannas —almost treeless, grassland patches in the jungle. An hour's flight north of Guatemala City, the great lake of Petén-Itzá comes into view, with smaller lakes, to the east of it. The dramatic island city of Flores lies in the southern part of this two part lake. It was here that the Maya of this area were finally subdued in battle with the Spaniards in 1697. The plane lands at the International Airport of Santa Elena, on the mainland south of Flores, where the visitor, if he has not done so already, can make arrangements for tourist services and transportation to Tikal according

Lake Petén Itzá and city of Flores with causeway leading from Santa Elena.

to the length of his stay. There is a regularly scheduled bus service to the site and taxis are likewise available. The distance from Santa Elena to Tikal is 64 Kms. by a good paved road.

In the National Park at Tikal there are accomodations for those who wish to spend a few days. The three existing hotels: "The Jungle Lodge", "Jaguar Inn", and "Tikal Inn" are located a short distance from the administrative offices. All three have restaurant service. There are several lunch rooms nearby and the Park also has a very pleasant camping area. Much can be seen by the visitor who comes into Tikal only for the day but of course, if one has the time, an overnight stay at least is preferable. Many people plan to spend at least three days in order to see not only the temples, palaces, and monuments, but the forest and all that it contains. The small museum near the airfield displays much of the material recovered by the archeologists. The forest with its exotic plant and animal life offers another aspect of Tikal, especially in the early morning and late afternoon. Hunting is not permitted at Tikal, which is a wildlife preserve; dogs and firearms are not allowed within the park.

Clothing at Tikal ought to be appropriate for the tropics and for day-long tramping and climbing. ladies will not be hindered by skirts but very tight ones are not advisable. An insect repellent is suggested. During the almost guaranteed dry months of February into May rain wear is unnecessary. However, December through February can have

Heron catching fish, from a pottery vessel, A.D. 800.

surprisingly cold, damp early mornings, and warm clothing, such as a heavy sweater or jacket, makes all the difference. The months of June into October, or so, are delightful, for everything comes back to life after the dry spells of April and May. While usually heavy when they come, infrequent rains merely enhance the beauty of Tikal. During March and April, when temperatures are at their maximum, the trees lose much of their foliage. This however is the time when the tops of the forest bloom with yellow, red, and lavender flowers.

The richness of the forest in the area of Tikal ranges from huge trees with mature heights of up to 150 feet, such as the magnificent Spanish cedars, the *ceibas* (a sacred tree to the Maya), the mahoganies, and the *zapotes* (the sap of which is the base of chewing gum) to a great variety of low and high palms. Pendant and looped throughout the forest are endless lianas, some covered with needle-like spines, others containing potable water (yet the trick is to cut this vine, the *bejuco de agua*, in a way so as not to lose the water within it). Two hundred and eighty-five species of birds have been recorded to date at Tikal. Of these, 209 are resident species. Among them are blue and white herons, hawks, parrots (almost always raucously overhead), golden turkeys, buzzards, *motmot* (a Bird of Paradise), even myriads of multicolored humming-birds. Large bands of spider monkeys populate Tikal. In late afternoons they can be seen moving from tree to tree throughout the central part of the ruins searching for food, especially the fruit of the *ramon* tree. Howler monkeys (aptly named) are rare today at Tikal following their decimation by disease in 1958. Beyond the Tikal settlement are plentiful jaguar, puma, and ocelot, as well as peccary, small deer (the brocket and Virginia deer) and, as one might expect, snakes, for the most part

Young spider monkeys.

harmless but harboring the venomous coral and fer-de-lance. The latter fortunately avoid archaeologists, workmen, and visitors. It is principally the awesome jaguar and the fer-de-lance (locally known as *barba amarilla*, after its yellow jaw) that the ancient Maya made so much of in their religion. These animals reappear throughout the art of Tikal, binding the past and present. Their representation in Tikal art tells us that the forest 1,500 years ago was very much what it is today. That the environment has been essentially continuous is further illustrated by the use of *zapote* and logwood in the lintels across doorways of Tikal buildings and by the presence of the heron in certain scenes portrayed in its art.

The massive ruins of Tikal are concentrated at the center of the Tikal National Park, a carefully preserved area of 222 square miles. This is the first such park in Central America. The Director of the National Park, under the Institute of Anthropology and History of Guatemala, supervises the maintenance of roads and trails and the consolidated and restored portions of the ruins, and also guards the flora and wildlife of Tikal. The site is laced with roads and trails, well marked by the Park, that lead to all the major archaeological groups.

The Tikal Museum was completed in 1964 through Guatemalan and foreign subscription. Housed in the Museum, a large patio-type structure, is a representative collection of objects of pottery, bone, shell, and stone, particularly jade, discovered in the work of the "Tikal Project," the archaeological group of the University Museum of the University of Pennsylvania, responsible for the excavations and architectural solidifications at the site between 1956 and 1969. The Tikal Museum was constructed and the exhibits installed to provide the visitor with a basis for appreciating the range, versatility, and beauty of the products of the Maya of Tikal. The materials have been arranged where possible in chronological order. Notably absent are objects of metal. The Maya of

*Pottery bowl with
painted fish, A.D. 650.*

Tikal flourished without gold and built what they did without metal tools (and, incidentally, without beasts of burden). That they accomplished so much with only chipped and ground stone tools is a striking fact of ancient Maya life here and elsewhere. Among the objects on exhibition are various stelae and altars removed from the ruins for reasons of preservation. A number of objects from the Museum's collections are shown in this guide. When available, publications dealing with Tikal can be purchased at the Museum.

All excavated material enters the laboratory where it is washed, sorted, and catalogued. It is stored after full study in a building constructed for that purpose. The archaeological materials belong to the Government of Guatemala and the very finest and most representative are transferred to the Tikal Museum for public exhibit. Water at Tikal, except for drinking water comes from an ancient reservoir, or aguada, filled by rain water, which was renovated by oil company bulldozers in 1958. Recently a water purifying system was installed by the Government. All hopes of gaining another source of water were abandoned in 1957 after several unsuccessful attempts at drilling. The fact is that the solid mantle of porous limestone underlying Tikal and practically all of the Petén retains water very poorly. There are no underground rivers or wells such as the *cenotes* in Yucatán.

Long-nosed god, a detail carved on the wooden lintel of Temple IV.

THE DISCOVERY OF TIKAL

The discovery of long-abandoned Tikal goes back more than a century. Actually, it was probably never lost. Guatemalan archives contain references to people moving to Tikal and living there in the 18th century. Very likely peoples living about Lake Petén-Itzá had always known of Tikal. But it was not until 1848 that an official expedition was made to the site. In 1853 an account of that trip was published in, of all places, a tome of the Berlin Academy of Science. This fascinating report describes the journey and explorations of Modesto Méndez and Ambrosio Tut, respectively commissioner and governor of El Petén of the times. Accompanying them was an artist, Eusebio Lara, who fancifully but identifiably drew various of the stelae and lintels of Tikal. The description of the temples and other features was brief. Nonetheless, on its publication, it brought the site to the attention of those inclined to read a report in German on some remote and inaccessible place. Méndez is reputed to have returned to Tikal in 1852 though no record of his visit survives.

A Swiss. Dr. Gustav Bernoulli, traveled in 1877 to Tikal. He later commissioned people from Lake Petén-Itzá to return to the site and to remove various carved wooden lintels from across the doorways of

*A recent drawing of Stela 9, to left, and, alongside,
Lara's depiction of the same over a century ago.*

Temples I and IV. These lintels eventually reached Basel, Switzerland, where today they are preserved and exhibited in the Museum fur Völkerkunde.

Systematic exploration and recording of Tikal was begun by Alfred Percival Maudslay, the pioneering Englishman who was one of the first to bring so many Maya ruins to the attention of science. Oddly enough, John Lloyd Stephens and his artist companion, Frederick Catherwood, earlier explorers in the 1840's of great and justified fame, never visited Tikal. Apparently they had heard no word of it. Maudslay traveled to the site in 1881 and in 1882 and made the first map and plans of its major architectural features. His men chopped furiously to free many of the great temples of the forest. The result was Maudslay's splendid photographs. His account and views of temples and monuments were

*Personage with his intricate regalia. Detail of
Lintel 3 of Temple IV, now in Basel.*

Temple I, as cleared and photographed
by Maudslay over 100 years ago.

published in his monumental archaeological contribution to a truly
weighty series of publications called *Biologia Centrali-Americana.*

Teobert Maler, a cantankerous but observant and incomparably
energetic German, visited the site twice, in 1895 and 1904, in the course
of his far-ranging, successful exploratory travels in the Maya area for the
Peabody Museum of Harvard University. In all, he spent over three
months at Tikal, drawing and superbly photographing all that he could
find. His work has been invaluable to all who followed him. But Maler
refused to submit his overall map of the site to the museum authorities,
fearing that the publication of his Tikal work would financially profit
the PeabodyMuseum (probably no museum has ever gained anything
much in the way of profits from its publications). This map has never
been found. A few years later the Museum was forced to field a special
expedition to make a new map and to complete the recording of Tikal, as

15

then known. This expedition consisted of Alfred Marston Tozzer, until his death in 1954 one of the greatest of Mayanists, and his assistant, R. E. Merwin. The two spent one month at the site and emerged with the map and additional data. A handsome, joint report, by Maler and Tozzer, was finally published in 1911 by the Peabody Museum.

With this report and that by Maudslay as a firm base, the pace of modern study of the site was quiet but progressive, largely through the interests of Sylvanus G. Morley (after whom the Tikal Museum has been named). Morley's particular concern was for Maya writing and his four visits to the site (1914, 1921, 1922, 1928) were devoted to recording the inscriptions on the Tikal monuments, as part of a then thorough compendium of such material for the whole of El Petén. Morley was head of the archaeological research program of the Carnegie Institution of Washington. From 1926 to 1937 Morley's archaeologists conducted excavations on a then unheard-of scale at the site of Uaxactun, five hours north of Tikal by foot. Here in Petén the work at Uaxactun yielded a basic understanding of ancient cultural development that has formed an essential guidepost in all subsequent excavations in the Maya area.

In 1956 the University Museum of the University of Pennsylvania inaugurated an 11-year program of study and excavation of Tikal. At that time the Museum signed a contract with the Government of Guatemala, and the Tikal Project was born. Edwin M. Shook, who had long worked at Uaxactun and other Maya centers as a Carnegie archaeologist, had for years enthusiastically advocated an intensive study of Tikal in all its aspects. Visiting Tikal from Uaxactun in 1937, Mr. Shook discovered two causeways converging on a new important group of ruins at the site (the so-called North Zone). He returned in 1942 to gather data for a now famed restoration drawing of Temple II by Tatiana Proskouriakoff, published in her splendid work, *An Album of Maya Architecture.* Mr. Shook in 1956 was appointed the first Field Director of the newly formed Tikal Project.

Without the cooperation of the Government of Guatemala, especially in its generous provision of air transport of materials and personnel (through the Air Force and Aviateca), the Tikal Project would have been seriously handicapped. With the continuous aid of the Guatemalan Government, the Tikal Project was able to field thirteen seasons of work (Jan. 1956 - Dec. 1969). Most important was the counsel of the Institute of Anthropology and History of Guatemala, under the direction of Don Carlos Samayoa Chinchilla. Funds for the work at Tikal were provided from many private, government, and foundation sources. Average annual expenditures amounted to over one hundred thousand dollars. From July of 1964 to December of 1969 the Guatemalan Government provided large sums through its Petén development agency, FYDEP, to allow more excavation and to consolidate and restore many buildings, thus enhancing the site for visitors.

The original aims of the Tikal Project, as conceived in 1956 by Froelich G. Rainey, the director of the University Museum, and by three of its board members, Percy C. Madeira, Jr., John Dimick, and Samuel B.

Eckert, long enthusiast of the Maya, were: to restore and preserve some of the world's most awesome architecture; to use techniques of modern archaeology in working out the history of the rise and fall of this great site; to establish a permanent field laboratory for the world's scholars and students of archaeology, anthropology, and American history; to open an almost primeval forest to scientists concerned with plant, animal, and bird life, geology, and climate; and to provide for sightseers a monument to America. Whether these goals have been met, only the visitor and scholar can judge.

In 1970 the "Tikal National Park Archaeological Project" was created with Guatemalan personnel, its principal object being the conservation of the site already restored and the opening up of other areas to visitors. Principally important among these areas is the so-called Group G which resulted in the publication of: "Reportes de las Investigaciones Arqueológicas en el Grupo 5E-11 Tikal" by Rudy Larios and Miguel Orrego, Guatemalan technicians trained by the University of Pennsylvania (1982).

Between the years 1979 and 1985 the Tikal National Project restored the Plaza of the Lost World and the North Zone. Although the work realized by these three projects is extensive and extraordinary, the area uncovered and restored is but a small part compared to what the jungle still holds.

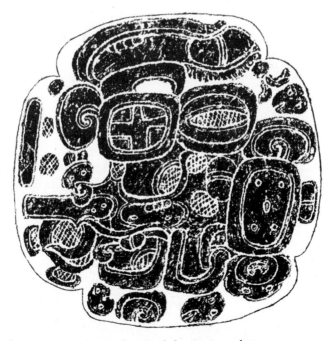

Rubbing of carved design on a large vessel found in a Late Classic burial.

Architectural complex of the Main Plaza, including the North Acropolis in the background, Temple I and part of the Central Acropolis

THE RUINS

Visitors to Tikal often find it difficult to plan their time to best advantage. A three-day visit is about ideal if one wishes to see everything and climb various of the great temples. However, much can be seen with an overnight stay, for example, a Twin-pyramid group, the Great Plaza and everything that bounds it, with time for the climb to the summit of Temple IV. For those who prefer to walk, leisurely walking times between major features of the site are listed here:

Museum to Great Plaza via Méndez Causeway: 20 minutes
Museum to Temple of the Inscriptions: 20 minutes
Museum to North Zone via Group E and Maler Causeway: 20 minutes
Great Plaza to the Temple of the Inscriptions: 20 minutes
Great Plaza to Temple IV: 10 minutes
Great Plaza to Plaza of the Seven Temples: 10 minutes
Temple IV to North Zone via Maudslay Causeway: 15 minutes
North Zone to Temple I via Maler Causeway: 15 minutes
Great Plaza to Group 5E-11 (Group G): 10 minutes
Great Plaza to "Lost World": 10 minutes

Large elaborate incense burner, A.D. 800.

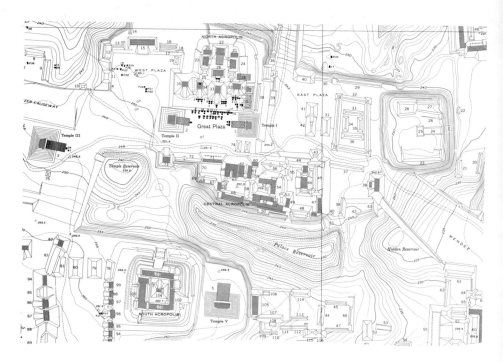

*A part of the mapa of Central Tikal which covers in its entirety
16 square kilometers or about 6 square miles (compare with map on p. 108).*

*A detailed map of the very center of Tikal, with surveyed
square 5D to the left and 5E to the right, each 500 meters on a side.*

What actually is Tikal? Sixteen square kilometers, or about six square miles of central Tikal have been mapped, revealing over 3,000 separate constructions: temples, palaces, shrines, ceremonial platforms, small to middling residences, ballcourts, terraces, causeways, plazas both small and huge, even a structure built for ritual sweat-bathing. Concentrated in and about the ceremonial precincts of the city are over 200 stone monuments, by which we mean sculptured and plain stelae and altars. These are vertically set shafts of stone and round, drum-shaped stones, usually paired. Burials and ritually cached offerings have been found by the hundreds, as have chultuns (subterranean chambers of enigmatic function excavated in bedrock). Perhaps as many as 10,000 earlier platforms and buildings lie sealed beneath the surface features mapped during 1957 to 1960. Excavations have revealed at least 1,100 years of apparently ceaseless construction. Stone monuments were erected at the site for 900 to 1,000 years. Over 100,000 tools, ceremonial objects, personal ornaments, and other items have been unearthed during the work of the Tikal Project. A million-odd potsherds, so important for establishing sequence and relative dating, have been collected in the course of the work.

Such statistics only hint at the enormity and richness of Tikal, especially when it is realized how small a percentage of Tikal has been excavated. Miles of ruin-packed territory are being studied, mapped and tested by digging in the area surrounding that part of Tikal seen by the visitor. It would easily require 20 more years of heavy work to investigate satisfactorily all the mapped, surface-situated construction covering central Tikal alone, and a century or so to know what these features overlie. Tikal is much like an iceberg with its bulk invisible beneath what we see on the surface. However it is not always necessary to dig a surface mound to be able to know with some confidence what it conceals. One can often calculate closely what is interred beneath the mound by the dimensions, form, and location of the mound, itself the product of the natural disintegration and collapse of, for example, a building with a stairway, walls, vaults, and roof. Yet Tikal is outstanding for the number of room walls and vaults still standing, as the visitor to the Plaza of the Seven Temples can appreciate. This high degree of preservation is a credit to the builders of Tikal. The vine-covered tree-infested temples and palaces so frequently encountered at Tikal have stood this way for almost a millennium.

It is well then to keep in mind that the majority of Tikal's buildings have subsided to mere mounds. Others still stand, only partly ruined, while others, found as mounds and as partially intact structures, have been cleared and repaired. Almost wherever one walks there are vestiges of earlier construction buried beneath one's feet: the floors of plazas and platforms, perhaps even a razed palace.

As he stands among the ruins of Tikal, the visitor experiences an understandable sense of disorientation. Without a feeling for time and

21

Excavation of a Late Classic tomb, Burial 77, in the West Plaza.

Temple IV rising above the tree tops.

The Main Plaza. Temple I facing Temple II in the foreground.

development and for the purpose of all the construction facing one, Tikal remains for most a hodgepodge of disconnected dates and things. Time, perhaps more than any other factor, can be the most bewildering in an archaeological setting. Fortunately for visitor and archaeologist alike a fairly simple sequential scheme exists to aid orientation:

A *Preclassic Period* began at Tikal about 600 B.C., if not earlier, and in this scheme, gave way to a *Classic Period* at about A.D. 250. The

A photo taken from a helicopter in 1966 which shows some of the archaeological evidence for the view shown on page 26, which is a reconstruction by H. Stanley Loten of the ceremonial heart of Tikal at about A.D. 800.
Seen from the north, this view includes Temple I, the Central Acropolis, and the North Acropolis (foreground) as well as distant groups to the south.

Classic Period is subdivided into an *Early Classic Period*, from A.D. 250 to 550, and a *Late Classic Period*, from A.D. 550 to the collapse of Tikal, about A.D. 900. At this point in time the *Postclassic Period* begins. The Preclassic era was one of development of Maya patterns of living and building during which many of the characteristics of Maya civilization were formed. During Classic times this civilization matured and crystallized and the site of Tikal grew spatially and architecturally to its final Late Classic magnificence. The majority of visible construction at Tikal dates from Classic times, particularly the Late Classic era (A.D. 550 to 900). Though still little understood, something happened around A.D. 900 and Classic life ceased. However, lingering Postclassic peoples continued to live and worship about the center of Tikal in the centuries following A.D. 900.

An understanding of what is known of Tikal history requires the use of such terms as Preclassic (some prefer Formative) and Classic (as we have just done) and, further, requires basic agreement as to what they mean roughly in time and achievement. Such terms are part of the language of maya archaeology. Additionally, they have temporal meaning throughout Mesoamerica, from northern Mexico southeast to Honduras and El Salvador.

The repair of excavated buildings at Tikal has taken two forms. The most common has been consolidation by which the ancient masonry is reinforced to prevent further deterioration. Restoration has also been practiced, in which masonry blocks have to be made and replaced where fallen in order to give a well-reasoned appearance of the original. Often both approaches are used on a single structure but always there has been an attempt to preserve the effect of a ruin with the clarity that only repair can give.

Great Plaza

It is about one mile on foot or by car from the Museum and the adjacent Jungle Inn to the Great Plaza, unquestionably the heart of ancient Tikal, with a history stretching back into the pre-Christian era. The visitor reaches the Great Plaza either south down the Maler Causeway, or from another direction, northwest up the steeply graded Méndez Causeway (see map). In either case, the proximity of the Great Plaza and all that architecturally bounds it, is announced by the view of the back of Temple I rising about 170 feet above the vast East Plaza. Where once broad stairs climbed up to the Great Plaza, a road now runs along the edge of the Central Acropolis and past a small ballcourt. Those who have worked at Tikal for years still continue to be awed by the architectural immensity and staggered masses of Tikal concentrated about the great expanse of this very center of Tikal. To the right, Temple I looks to the west across the Plaza to the balancing Temple II. To the north is the North Terrace stairway, 230 feet in length, and behind the Terrace the clustered temples of the North Acropolis. Seventy stelae and altars occur in rows and groups in the Plaza and on the Terrace.

The Great Plaza consists of four superimposed floors of plaster, each covering an area of about two and one-half acres. The combined thickness of these averages 15 inches while limestone bedrock is only two feet beneath one's feet under much of the Plaza. The earliest plaza floor is estimated to have been laid about 150 B.C. and the latest at about A.D. 700. These four plaster surfaces successively witnessed the ceremonial drama of Tikal which was played over almost a thousand years.

Temple I

By now almost a hallmark of Tikal, this magnificently proportioned structure is popularly known as the Temple of the Giant Jaguar after a motif on one of its carved lintels. It is technically designated as Structure 5D-1 (that is to say, the first numbered structure in Square 5D-500 meters on a side, on the map of central Tikal). This incomparable example of Maya architecture, executed in limestone, was built about A.D. 700, midway in Late Classic times. Its roof comb towers about 145 feet above the Great Plaza. The huge, pyramidal substructure with its nine sloping terraces (the number 9 was sacred to the Maya) supports, first, a building platform which, in turn, serves as a base for a three-room temple, each room set behind the other in tandem fashion. The ornamental roof comb, perched on the temple roof, was built in two distinct levels, with a hollow, vaulted chamber sealed within each level to reduce the weight of the whole. The face of the roof comb is finished with stone blocks arranged to form a monumentally proportioned seated individual flanked by elaborate scrolls and suggestions of serpents. Discouragingly eroded, this enthroned ruler can be discerned in the sunlight of early afternoon. This tableau, in fact the whole roof comb, was probably once contrastingly painted in cream, red, and other colors, perhaps green and blue. Elsewhere at Tikal there is evidence that whole temples were once painted red.

The stair which one climbs to the summit of Temple I was built by the Maya during and in order to complete the construction of Temple I. It is spoken of as a "construction stairway" and up it were carried the tons of lime mortar, fill, and masonry blocks employed to complete the temple standing on the pyramid proper. The final stair, up which the priests must have labored in their opulent costumes, was made of large, deeply tenoned blocks, heavily plastered. This stair is preserved as a remnant at the level of the Great Plaza.

Temple I embodies all the traits of traditional Maya temple construction. These characteristics include the pyramidal, heavily terraced substructure, with complicated insets and changes of the levels of the moldings decorating each terrace (the ins and outs, ups and downs, and deliberate accentuation of all of this through shadow must impress anyone architecturally acute); a stair spanning the pyramid from top to bottom; a building platform on which the building itself rests; a building exteriorly comprising two obvious parts, a higher and narrower portion to the rear, separated from the front portion by narrow indentations at the sides, as if two houses built at different levels had been joined; and a high roof comb set to the rear of the building.

In the case of Temple I, the three temple chambers are narrow and spanned by high corbelled vaults. This is the famed Maya arch, formed by inclining or cantilevering two opposed wall faces and closing the gap at the top of these faces with a row of horizontally laid capstones. Each vault, of deeply tenoned, specially cut masonry blocks, is spanned by horizontal rows of round wooden beams, called vault beams, which simulate the crossbeams found in Maya bush houses. These and the wooden lintels in Temple I are made of *zapote* (elsewhere at Tikal we see, in addition to zapote, such woods as *habin* and logwood), the exceptionally hard, red-brown, rot-resistant wood of the sapodilla tree growing throughout much of the Petén forest. Tikal is famed for its superb, fantastically carved wooden lintels, many of which were removed by Bernoulli and others for preservation in museums (London, Basel, and New York). The three doorways of Temple I were spanned by multi-beamed lintels placed in beds at the tops of the walls. The outer doorway has a plain lintel (the apparent rule at Tikal). Two carved beams of the original four-beam lintel across the middle doorway are still in place (the whereabouts of the other two carved beams, removed in the 19th century, remains a mystery). In the proper afternoon light if one looks up, one can discern an intricate scene of a seated priest, over whom looms an enormous stylized serpent. An epoxy resin cast from molds made of these beams in Basel and London has been affixed to the underside of the new concrete beams. On entering the outer rooms and looking up one can make out a series of red imprints of human hands. These may have been made by Postclassic people, though their purpose is not known.

Beneath the floor at the center of the rear room archaeologists in 1958 discovered a deep pit leading down to a grave of an important individual buried after the temple had been built but prior to A.D. 900. The deeply set grave had been broken into by Maya still using the temple as a place of worship as late as the 12th, even 13th century. The pit they dug was filled with broken pottery incense burners, copal (their sacred incense gum), as well as the bones of one of their own people who had recently died.

Many wonder what is inside the towering Temple I pyramid. First of all, it consists of solid, increasingly massive construction cores with

Seated, gesturing lord on a vase from Burial 116. A.D. 790. ——▶

Bone carved with silhouetted face above a demon, found in Burial 116. Length of whole object, 10 inches.

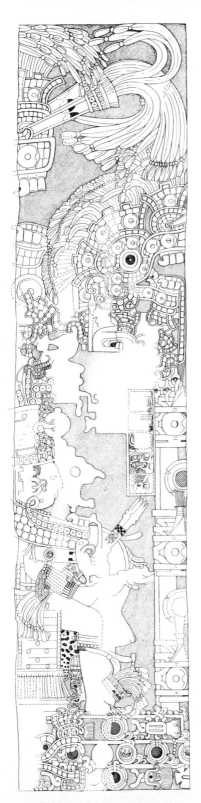

*Still in place,
the surviving two beams
of the lintel above
the middle doorway
of Temple I.*

their own specialized stairs. The many stages by which the Maya built Temple I were partially revealed by excavating tunnels within the pyramid. It was during such tunneling that one of the richest of the known Late Classic tombs of Tikal was found. Known prosaically as Burial 116, the grave was a large vaulted chamber made within a 20-foot deep excavation into the Great Plaza immediately before commencing the building of Temple I. The vaulted chamber measured 14 $\frac{1}{2}$ by 8 feet, and was 13 feet high within. All but 2 $\frac{1}{2}$ feet of the floor area was occupied by a rectangular masonry bench. On this bench, with his head to the north, was the skeleton of a large man extended full length on his back. As a capstone across the vault was removed by Aubrey S. Trik, (who, with George F. Guillemin, was responsible for the many restorations at Tikal), and a light thrust in, the sight was disappointing because portions of the chamber had anciently collapsed, covering the rich interment. Days of painstaking clearing and work with small brushes and delicate probes resulted in the uncovering of the fabulous outlay of jades, pearls, pottery, alabaster, and orange-red shells from the Pacific, all about and around the skeleton. The body evidently had been laid out on a woven mat fringed with jade beads and spiny oyster shells. Some 180 pieces of worked jade adorned the body; consisting of necklaces, ear ornaments, bracelets, anklets, the headdress and mat fringes, the total weighed 16 $^{1}/_{2}$ pounds. Large polychrome jars and plates, one in the form of a sectioned conch shell, lay on the bench and in the aisle. Also on the floor of the tomb in one corner was a heap of bone fragments, 90 in all. Some of these were carved with hieroglyphic inscriptions and others with beautifully rendered scenes of canoes filled with dieties. The designs were incised on a flattened surface of the bone and the lines filled with cinnabar. There were thirty-seven pieces thus engraved. (There is a replica of this tomb in the Tikal Museum where most of the objects described here are displayed. Some pieces too crushed and warped to be restored are not in view).

How are features like Temple I and the tomb dated? This is frequently a complicated matter, involving various approaches. We know, for instance, after a great deal of excavation, that Temple I is a few years younger than Temple II, across the way, because Temple I sits on the same Plaza floor that abuts the base of Temple II. This is an example of relative dating. On occasion it is possible to link a structure, such as Temple I, to a stela that carries the date of its erection in Maya notation or to a lintel which carries a similar notation. It is therefore possible to say that a structure was built or occupied at a certain point in Maya time. It then becomes a question of translating Maya to Christian time. Various correlation schemes exist (see Appendix). Obviously only one can be correct. The pottery within the tomb, for instance in Burial 116, can help in relative dating. The sequence of major types of pottery has been worked out through years of excavation here and elsewhere in the Maya area. The pottery in Burial 116 is stylistically Late Classic. Therefore, Temple I is Late Classic, certainly no earlier than this because pottery of that period was already in existence at the time of building. Similarly, the forms of masonries used, their pattern of installation, and a myriad of construction details also point to Temple I as Late Classic. However, we are after real dates in Christian time. Actually it was Temple I that helped to pin down which of the proposed Maya-Christian correlations is correct.

The radiocarbon, or C-14 method of dating was used on the lintels and vault beams to determine when the beams were cut and installed. In the case of Temple I the results indicated a construction date of about A.D. 700, which confirmed dating provided by relative means. Within Temple IV archaeologists chose for radiocarbon testing a number of samples of various vault beams and a wooden lintel on

Temple II and, in the distance, Temple IV ——▶

Stela 22, with a date of A.D. 771.

which what has been interpreted as its date of installation had been carved. This Maya date is equivalent to A.D. 741, using the 11.16.0.0.0 Correlation (see Appendix). The results of testing fell between A.D. 712 and 780. This experiment confirmed the unlikelihood of any other correlation being the correct one. In other words, Maya dates on lintels and stone monuments could be translated into Christian time with increased confidence. These dates might then be applied to buildings to which the monuments and carved lintels related. These are examples of relative and absolute methods of dating used to work out the chronology of events at Tikal and elsewhere.

Tikal buildings referred to as temples seem appropriately designated. They are high, remote, and thus suitable for ceremonies and even the astronomical pursuits of the priests. Temples dominate great public plazas where the populace assembled to witness priestly processions up the stairs to the chambers far above and closed from their view. The buildings appear to have been religious precincts within which the theocrats interceded with the gods of rain, sun, wind, and corn through the use of incense, incantation, and calculation. Frequently signs of ritual burning of incense occur within the rooms and on the stairs. How much human sacrifice was carried out publicly or secretively within and outside these chambers is difficult to guess. Individuals were definitely decapitated at Tikal, and it is absolutely certain that the Tikal Maya did inter attendants in burials of many of the elite. The gory, supremely devotional acts of the Maya at the time of the Conquest, and especially of the Aztec of Central Mexico, cannot be verified here for earlier times. Elaborate state burials of important individuals often took place prior to the construction of the pyramidal base upon which the temples were set. A later burial intruded into this pyramid often called for the renewal of the temple building.

Temple II

Temple II, across the Plaza from Temple I, is in many ways a squat version of Temple I. Known as the Temple of the Masks after its richly embellished façade, Temple II consists of a three-terraced pyramid on which rests a large platform. The stairway on the front of this platform is flanked by a pair of large, grotesque masks, only vague details of which survive. This platform supports the building platform which in turn sustains the temple building itself. Today Temple II stands about 125 feet high above the Great Plaza though its original height with its intact roof comb must have been close to 140 feet. Temple II, like Temple I, has three rooms. Again one steps up going from room to room through the narrow vaulted chambers. Oddly, the outer and inner doorways were spanned by uncarved lintels while the central lintel was carved. One of the original five beams of this central lintel fortunately survives in the American Museum of Natural History in New York. A large masonry block had been built in front of the temple building. This has been restored. It has been speculated that this block served as a sort of reviewing stand, as the angle of its placement allowed the priests standing on it to be seen by the populace in the Plaza below, and vice-versa. The extravangly adorned roof comb of Temple II features a ruined central face flanked by elaborate earplugs, or circular ornaments. Within the massive roof comb are various superimposed sealed chambers. The temple dates from about the time of Temple I, or about A.D. 700. A fascinating feature of this structure is the myriad incised drawings, or graffiti, covering portions of the walls of the rooms. Of special note among the graffiti are scenes of temples, and even a tableau of a bound victim being impaled by a spear thrown by a masked individual. Some of these graffiti were almost certainly done during the Classic Period, but one suspects that others were done in early Postclassic times. The walls also retain more recent and destructive names, initials and other mementos of visitors, senselessly destroying this valuable record of the past. Park laws prohibit the defacement of monuments and buildings.

All of Temple II above its pyramidal substructure has been cleared of debris and consolidated. Fallen lintels have been replaced and the stairs and stair block in front of the building have been restored. The largest monument at Tikal, the uncarved Stela P83 (originally 11 feet 8 inches high), and its accompanying altar were found shattered at the base of the pyramid stair. They have now been restored.

Plaza and Terrace Monuments

The many stelae and altars found in two rows in the Great Plaza and in groups on the North Terrace are particularly interesting. Excavation has shown that over 40 percent of them owe their positions to the revivalistic efforts of Postclassic peoples who survived the breakdown of Classic control around A.D. 900. To take an example, the front or south row of monuments in the Great Plaza, four equally spaced stela-altar units, was placed there during Late Classic times (represented by Stelae P22-P27). All other monuments in the row were added in Postclassic times. A dramatic instance is Stela P21, the second from the left in the row. This had been originally erected in a row of monuments in the West Plaza northwest of Temple II. It was broken and its top two-thirds was transported some 330 feet into the Great Plaza and re-erected where it may be found today. To serve as an altar for this stela, these Postclassic peoples recovered from an ancient dump the lower portion of the Early Classic Stela 2, which they then trimmed as a block, added some lines, and placed in front of the stela. The top portion of Stela 2 was hauled up onto the North Acropolis -quite a task—and re-erected in the sunken court in front of Structure 5D-26.

Each stela and altar at Tikal has its Project-assigned number painted in red on it on the side or rear base. Plain monuments have the prefix "P." Carved monuments in the Great Plaza are of Tikal are as follows:

Monument	Location	Maya Date	Equivalent date
Stela 3	In front of Structure 5D-34	9.2.13.0.0	Early Classic, A.D. 488
Stela 4	Ibid.	8.17.10.0.0(?)	Early Classic, possibly A.D. 386
Altar 1	Ibid.	?	Probably Late Classic
Stela 5 and Altar 2	In front of Structure 5D-33	9.15.13.0.0	Late Classic, A.D. 744
Stela 6	In front of Structure 5D-32	9.4.0.0.0	Early Classic, A.D. 514
Altar 3	Ibid.	?	Early Classic, about A.D. 500
Altar 12	Ibid. (Now Tikal Museum)	?	Early Classic, about A.D. 500
Stela 7	In front of Structure 5D-29	9.3.0.0.0	Early Classic, A.D. 495
Stela 8	Rear row, Great Plaza, west	?	Early Classic, about A.D. 500
Stela 18	Ibid.	8.18.0.0.0(?)	Early Classic, possibly A.D. 396
Stela 9	Rear row, Great Plaza, center	9.2.0.0.0	Early Classic, A.D. 475
Stela 10	Ibid.	?	Early Classic, about A.D. 550
Stela 11 and Altar 11	Ibid.	10.2.0.0.0	Late Classic, A.D. 869
Stela 12	Rear row, Great Plaza, east	9.4.13.0.0	Early Classic, A.D.527
Stela 13	Ibid.	?	Early Classic, about A.D. 500
Stela 14	Ibid.	?	Early Classic, about A.D. 525

Various carved monuments in this series are of particular interest. The long glyphic inscription on the sides of Stela 5 is considered by many to be the most beautifully executed in the Maya area. Stela 11 is the latest at Tikal. Stela 14 is remarkable in that it is a small fragment that was re-erected backwards in Postclassic times, having been intruded into the Late Classic North Terrace stairway. Stela 7 was found as a mass of small and large fragments, only the lower portion could be successfully reconstructed and it has been set in a spot about where it was found. Stela 4 was discovered by Maler standing upside down, the position chosen for it when re-erected by Postclassic peoples.

As a rule Early Classic monuments throughout Tikal are smaller and less symmetrically shaped that Late Classic ones. Late Classic stelae often resemble round-topped tombstones. The stone of Late Classic monuments is either dolomite or dolomitic limestone and is distinguished by marked bedding planes. In contrast, Early Classic monuments were made of true limestone which here has an almost flint-like quality with a tendency to break conchoidally. Frequently this limestone is naturally pitted. Weathering hollows out these pits even further, often destroying the carving.

Monuments now without carving are believed to have always been plain. No signs have been found of stucco being applied to them to simulate carving. Probably all carved monuments and lintels, if not the plain ones as well, were painted red by the Maya at Tikal. Definite traces of red paint have been found on some protected monuments and lintels. Both plain and sculptured stelae were originally provided with cached offerings about and under their bases. These offerings consisted of exotically chipped pieces of flint and obsidian (the so-called "eccentrics"), sea shells, and other strange items. As a rule, caches with Late Classic stelae were composed of nine eccentric flints and nine flakes of obsidian on which the same set of deities was repeatedly incised. Examples of these offerings are on display in the Tikal Museum.

The Tikal Maya normally placed an altar with a stela. If the stela was carved, the altar was carved. The pair was placed in a prominent position, usually directly in front of a temple pyramid. The Great Plaza rows of monuments, as arranged in Classic times, were apparently dedicated to the myriad temples comprising the North Acropolis. Study has shown that stelae and altars were repeatedly and deliberately broken up during Classic times. Carved ones were not erected as permanent time-markers whose inscriptions could endlessly be consulted. Permanent records must have been kept in folded books by the priests and their scribes. Three such Maya codices, but from much later times in Yucatán, survive in European libraries. Postclassic peoples appear to have retrieved various monument fragments from Classic dumps for their own peculiar cult purposes. The Classic Maya, in breaking a monument, took care to smash the face of the individual or priest depicted on it, as if to kill the stela and what it portrayed. This

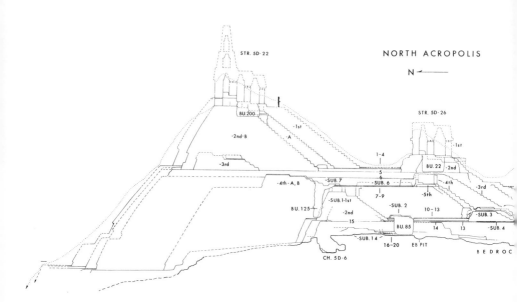

STR. 5D-22

BU.200

-1st

-2nd-B

A

STR. 5D-26

1st

1-4

-3rd

BU. 22 -2nd

5

6

-4th-A, B

-SUB. 7

-SUB. 6

-4th

-3rd

-SUB.1-1st

7-9

-5th

BU.125

-2nd

-SUB. 2

10-13

-SUB. 3

15

BU.85

14

13

-SUB. 4

-SUB. 14

16-20

EB PIT

CH. 5D-6

BEDROC

A composite north-south section through the North Acropolis, covering a distance of almost 500 feet. About 1000 years of construction are represented here. Everything below Floor 5 is Preclassic and, above it, Classic, or after A.D. 250.

is a custom that survived, as the visitor will note the large number of smashed faces on monuments throughout the site which were never damaged during Classic times.

A frequent question is what do the carved figures represent. A Tikal stela commonly has a single standing personage, richly garbed and ornamented, on its front. There is increasing evidence that these are priestly individuals who successively, even jointly, ruled Tikal. It has been speculated that when a priest died, or a line of succession of related priests was broken or replaced, their monuments were sacrificed. Even their temples may have been ritually desecrated and razed. Then new ones were built over them. At other sites in the Maya area, study has recently shown the existence of birth dates and dates of accession to power on the stelae and lintels. All in all, while once monuments were thought to depict gods, or priests in the guise of gods, it is now increasingly probable that the majority show actual individuals who belonged to the ruling elite. Many Tikal monuments mark cyclical periods of time. But the question remains: To what do these points in time pertain? For the visitor interested in how the Maya calculated time and recorded it, a short account has been appended to this guide. This calculation is one of the most intriguing acomplishments of the lowland Classic Maya.

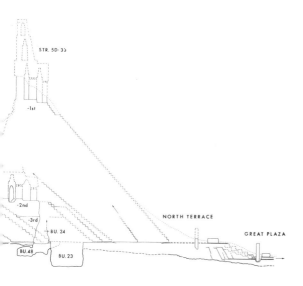

STR. 5D-33

-1st

-2nd

-3rd

BU. 24

BU. 48

BU. 23

NORTH TERRACE

GREAT PLAZA

North Acropolis

Directly linked by a series of floors to the long sequence of North Terrace stairs, the North Acropolis is the single most complex feature, from the standpoints of growth and content, yet excavated in the Maya area. With a base covering about two and a half acres, the top of the great platform of the Acropolis rests some 30 feet above limestone bedrock and about 40 feet above the Great Plaza. Solidly constructed throughout, the Acropolis must be thought of as a huge platform (of which the North Terrace is a part). Buildings were constructed on the top of this platform. What the visitor sees, impressive as it is, amounts to merely the final stage of the growth of the North Acropolis. There are buried within the Acropolis over a dozen earlier versions, one on top of the other. It required four long seasons of deep trenching into the mass of the Acropolis to expose something of its construction sequence. Vestiges of as many as 100 buildings lie buried in this mass, the earliest dating back to around 200 B.C. Pits cut into bedrock contained traces of occupation dating even four centuries earlier. Here, by 100 B.C. the Maya were constructing successive elaborate platforms that supported large temples decorated with beautifully modeled and poly-chromed stuccoed façades and huge masks flanking stairways. Architecture, ornamentation, and vaulted tombs from this era drama-tically illustrate the sophistication of Preclassic Tikal. Many of the items from these early tombs are exhibited in the Tikal Museum.

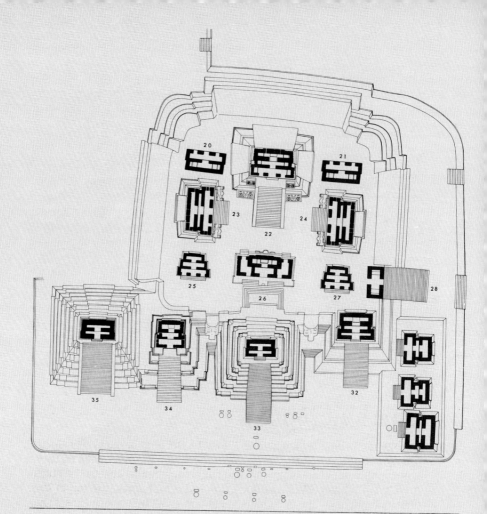

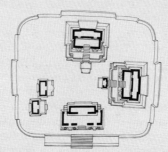

The upper plan is of the North Acropolis as it appeared finally in A.D. 800 though many details are not certain. The lower plan is of an earlier now deeply buried stage, from about A.D. 1. This stage appears in section with "Floor 10" in the drawing on pages 40 and 41.

(Left) Plan of Burial 166, 50 B.C. Such interments are a major source of information on the Preclassic Maya of Tikal. (Right) Masquette, 5 inches high, of soft green stone with eyes and teeth of inlaid shell. A.D. 1.

The consolidated and slightly restored Structure 5 D-23 built in the third century A.D., a superb example of early temple construction. In the right background is Structure 5D-22.

By about A.D. 250 the North Acropolis started to take on its now visible form. All buildings then extant were razed and a completely new Acropolis platform was built. Four vaulted buildings were then constructed on this platform. These are the partially revealed temple beneath Structure 5D-22 to the north center, 5D-23 on the west center of the Acropolis, 5D-24, its unexcavated twin to the east, and the now heavily restored 5D-26 in the center of the Acropolis. All appear to have functioned for religious, ceremonial ends. Each was rebuilt twice during Early Classic times with the exception of 5D-22, which consists of three superimposed temples. This Maya practice of building over the old is well shown by Structure 5D-22. Archaeologists have removed much of the west and northwest portions of the final version (built in the 5th century) in order to reveal the substructure and additions to it of an earlier temple, built about A.D. 350, and elaborately decorated with large plastered and painted masks. This temple in turn overlies a much smaller and entirely buried earlier one that was constructed about A.D. 250.

Eventually Structure 5D-25 and its balancing twin, 5D-27, came into being to the sides of the by then centuries old 5D-26. Excavation has shown that 5D-25 (and presumably its east twin) immediately overlies two prior Early Classic versions. Finally, at the northeast and northwest corners of the Acropolis, Structures 5D-20 and 21 were built facing to the north. It is estimated that these buildings came into being at about the end of Early Classic times, that is, about A.D. 550. It is clear that the symmetrically arranged buildings resting on the Acropolis are entirely Early Classic and those that we see were constructed over the course of three centuries. This is the single greatest concentration of Early Classic architecture visible today —an architecture characterized by many traits evident in the later Temples I and II on the Great Plaza. However, masonries differ greatly. In Early Classic times, building platforms were as a rule built as a finished unit, completely plastered, before the room walls were built upon the plastered floor. This and other traits of construction are peculiar to Early Classic times and with the ceramics and stone monuments of this era combine to give "Early Classic" a cultural make-up distinct from that of "Preclassic" and "Late Classic."

The North Acropolis, apart from being a massive platform covered by the temples just noted, includes three buildings added against its south face. A fine example of an Early Classic temple is Structure 5D-34, to the left as one views the North Acropolis from the Great Plaza. Nothing is simple in Maya building, for, as one stands today looking south from the rooms of 34, there is an excellent chance that a long history of construction lies beneath one's feet. A narrow trench was cut practically through the whole of this temple in 1959. Evidence of two earlier platforms, one on top of the other, was encountered in this work. At the deepest point of this trench the excavators discovered that the Maya, just prior to building the earliest platform, had cut a huge pit through the North Terrace down into bedrock. Within the hollowed-out bedrock, the Maya constructed a tomb which quickly received one of the goriest burials ever seen. Even as the bedrock walls were collapsing about them, the Maya buried one of their priests and with him, nine

44

*Part of the finely carved
hieroglyphic text of the
Early Classic Stela 26.*

retainers, necessarily killed for the occasion. Turtles and a crocodile were included in this bizarre tomb. A mass of beautifully painted pottery was included, much of it inspired by Teotihuacán, the hugely influential site of these fifth century times north of Mexico City. Many pieces from this tomb (Burial 10) are on exhibition in the Tikal Museum.

One of the most striking finds found in the room of Structure 34 was the incomplete Stela 26, known commonly as the Red Stela from the pigment preserved on it (this stela is also in the Tikal Museum). This beautiful Early Classic monument had stood nearby and had been deliberately shattered by the Maya, probably early in Late Classic times. Many of the weighty fragments were hauled up the stairway of 34 into the temple and laid to rest beneath a masonry altar specially constructed against the center of the rear wall to conceal the fragments. There they rested until Postclassic times, when vandals entered the chamber, smashed open the altar, and generally created havoc in the temple rooms. These same people appear to have been responsible

*One of the awesome masonry and plaster masks
that decorate the pyramid of Structure 5D-33-3rd.*

also for the looting of a, by then, 500-year old tomb in Structure 5D-26 up on the Acropolis, as well as of a less ancient tomb high up in the rooms of Structure 5D-22 to the rear of the Acropolis.

At the front-center of the North Acropolis is Structure 5D-33, probably the most intensively explored and excavated temple at Tikal, if not in the whole Maya area. Three structures, one over the other, are partially visible today. The latest is termed 33-1st. Originally the pyramid and its two-room building towered close to 110 feet. Built before Temples I and II, around A.D. 600, this great edifice was found to be discouragingly ruined when it was excavated in 1959 and 1960. Tree roots and time had largely denuded the pyramid of masonry. As if to compensate for the sad state of 33-1st, tunneling beneath it disclosed two magnificently embellished Early Classic temples, 33-2nd, and beneath it, 33-3rd.

A great many considerations entered into the decision to dismantle what was necessary of 33-1st to reveal the anciently mutilated but still impressively preserved earlier temples. Today, as one stands in the Great Plaza, one sees the lowest terraced parts of 33-1st wrapped about and over the rooms and supporting platform of 33-2nd. Fantastic masks decorate the facade of the temple proper, while others, monstrous heads with earplugs through which serpents twine, are seen on

(Left) The painted walls of Burial 48, with the central Maya date. These paintings were removed before this deep chamber was reburied. (Right) Probably the finest of the Tikal Early Classic pottery vessels, from this same burial. Diameter 6 inches.

the supporting platform to the sides of an access stairway. Still another platform underlies this one. This earliest platform is 33-3rd and once carried its own building, which was dismantled to make way for the platform of 33-2nd. The platform of 33-3rd is faced by two masks over ten feet high depicting long-nosed gods, one to the east and one to the west. Both are visible today by way of a system of tunnels and are among the most awesome sights of Tikal. Each owes its good preservation to the fact that the Maya covered them over with new masks at the time of building 33-2nd. But at the time of building 33-1st, these masks were brutally hacked and almost completely stripped of their red and white painted decorative plaster.

During the tunneling of Structure 5D-33, three tombs were encountered. The earliest of these, and Early Classic in time, was Burial 48. This was in a chamber cut into bedrock immediately before building the latest stairway from the North Terrace to the Acropolis (against this stairway 33-3rd was later built). This tomb yielded a wealth of fine material much of which is shown in the Tikal Museum. Most noteworthy were the chamber walls which were found covered by a painted hieroglyphic text including a Maya date corresponding to March 18, A.D. 457. Just before the abandonment of 33-2nd in the 8th century and the beginning of 33-1st, two important individuals died within a few weeks or months. To entomb the first, the Maya ripped out the whole center of the platforms of 33-2nd and -3rd, exposing the long-buried North Terrace floor. Through this an excavation was carried down into bedrock, a vaulted chamber with benches at its ends constructed, and this individual interred with his pots and jades. This tomb is known as Burial 23. The third burial, 24, was made at the bottom of a deep shaft cut down into the underlying platforms directly in front of the doorway of 33-2nd. In the interval between these two burials, Stela 31 was arduously worked up the stairs and re-erected in the rear chamber of 33-2nd.

Of all the finds at Tikal Stela 31 is surely one of the most extraordinary. In 1960, tunneling south from the Acropolis into 33, we found Stela 31 standing in the solidly filled rear room of 33-2nd. Stela 31, now standing in the Tikal Museum, is one of the finest Early Classic carvings ever found. Although burned and shattered by the Maya prior to building 33-1st, its protected position, sealed by the hearting of 33-1st, permitted the fascinating sculptured surfaces to survive. This limestone monument appears to have been ceremonially "killed," after having stood long at the base of 33-2nd. It was finally reset askew in a crude, specially excavated pit in the rear room of 33-2nd. The Maya burned the lower part of the stela here and went on to smash elaborate pottery incense burners about it, all as part of some enigmatic ceremony marking the end of both the stela and its temple. The vaults and roof comb were brought down and the construction of 33-1st begun. While the date of Stela 31 is still controversial within the 5th century, we can be sure of its sacrifice and burial in the 8th century.

The excavation of 33-1st has revealed important evidente of exactly how the Maya built it and other contemporary temples. A deceptively formal-looking flat-topped pyramid, 40 feet high, was thrown up over 33-2nd, completely burying it. A stair reached from the North Terrace to the top on its south side and permitted maya workmen to carry up the incalculable tons of mortar, mud, and rubble fill, as well as the stone blocks to retain this fill. When this core had been completed, it too was gradually interred beneath a second core with its own stairway, built in ever higher and narrower stages, eventually reaching a height of 62 feet. There is some evidence that the Maya, as they built each stage of this massive core, completed as well the masonry faces of the planned pyramid. Each level of this core and the one beneath it consists of dozens of walled-up blocks of fill. Most were rectangular but in the lower stages of the pyramid these were curved and some can be seen today radiating from the core-pyramid about 33-2nd. The effort that went into such construction staggers us and makes us ponder how it was all directed and achieved, and for what ends.

To the left of Structure 5D-34 and just north of Temple II is 35, a tall Late Classic temple built against the southwest corner of the North Acropolis. Very little remains of its once majestic narrow-roomed building. It has been barely touched by excavation.

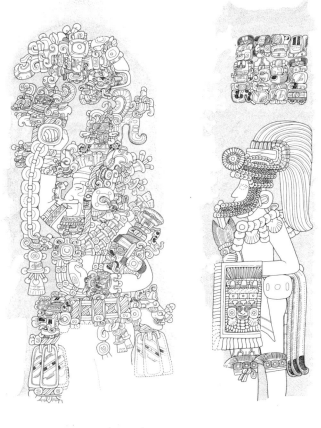

Stela 31 front and sides, and a photographic detail of the wonderfully preserved carving. The individuals on the sides carry spear-throwers and appear to be from central Mexico, perhaps Teotihuacán.

49

Immediately to the east of 33 is Structure 5D-32, partially cleared in 1965 and 1966. Ib belongs to Late Classic times, probably the early 7th century, placing it earlier than Temples I and II. The three huge rooms that comprise its building had been ransacked of offerings beneath the floors shortly following the collapse of Tikal in the 10th century. Tunneling at the base of the pyramid and on its center line failed to disclose a buried earlier structure. However, one of the most intriguing tombs ever found was discovered in tunneling, by following the outlines of the ancient excavation down deep into bedrock. There archaeologists discovered Burial 195, a vaulted chamber containing a single skeleton surrounded and overlying masterpieces of stucco-on-wood art. Perhaps the most exciting were four identical wooden figures covered by egg-shell thin light blue plaster, standing 15 inches high, and depicting the Maya rain-god. Elaborately plastered, carved and painted wooden boards were lying under the skeleton. Beautifully decorated pottery plates and even a stuccoed wooden throne and a pair of alabaster rodents surrounded the body. The wooden objects had rotted; but by injecting Plaster of Paris the archaeologists were able to capture the thin Maya plaster that had covered them originally. This tomb was made immediately prior to starting construction of the temple itself.

To the east of 32 and north of Temple I are three diminutive Early Classic temples facing west. While everything visible has been recorded, practically nothing is known of them through excavation. One can only wonder what wealth and detail they contain.

Great Plaza Ballcourt

The small ballcourt, Structure 5D-74, just south of Temple I, was built in Late Classic times and consists of two parallel constructions with a narrow, relatively short playing alley in between. This is one of the smallest courts known. A sloping bench occurs on either side of the alley and connects with the almost vertical wall, or apron, behind it. A narrow inset stair on both the north and south ends gave access to the top of each side of the court. No stone markers were found either in the alley or on the aprons. The game was played with a rubber ball by players wearing protective pads on their hips and knees but without using their hands. It was a highly ceremonial affair, judging from Spanish accounts of the game at the time of the Conquest. A triple ballcourt is known at Tikal (in the Plaza of the Seven Temples) and a third court is found in the East Plaza, behind Temple I.

Pyramid with Perishable Temple

At the southwest corner of the Great Plaza, just south of Temple II, stands a high steep pyramid, facing north, known as Structure 5D-73. The absence of debris on its top and at its base suggested to archaeolo-

Jade bead, 3 ¹/₂ inches long, with a Maya in a diving pose on each of its four sides. Burial 196, A.D. 700.

gists over the years that 73 was an example of a temple with a pole-and-thatch building on top, exactly as depicted in certain graffiti on the walls of Temple II. Excavations in 1965 and 1966 suggest that this could well have been the case. Axial tunneling of this Late Classic structure, in many ways like the pyramid of Temple I, yielded the sumptuous Burial 196, set beneath the Plaza level below the pyramid center. The single skeleton lay extended on a masonry bench along one side of the finely vaulted chamber. On the plastered bench and floor were scattered close to 50 pottery vessels, among them some of the loveliest polychrome, figure-painted pieces known. Because portions of the chamber had buckled and fallen, various items were crushed. Among the spectacular contents was a carved, possibly sleeping, jaguar of solid jade, weighing about 3 ¹/₂ pounds, the largest piece of carved jade known from Mesoamerica and now a prize exhibit in the Tikal Museum. From hundreds of beautifully fashioned pieces of jade a cylinder and lid on which was surmounted an elaborate human head was painstakenly restored. This jade mosaic vessel is surely one of the masterpieces of ancient world art. In many ways the contents and layout of this burial duplicate Burial 116 of Temple I, suggesting not only their contemporaneity but a close relationship between the individuals buried within them.

Drawings of designs on polychrome vessels discovered in Burial 196,
a tomb from A.D. 700. The small vase, only 5 inches high,
providing the uppermost design is shown in color on the opposite page.

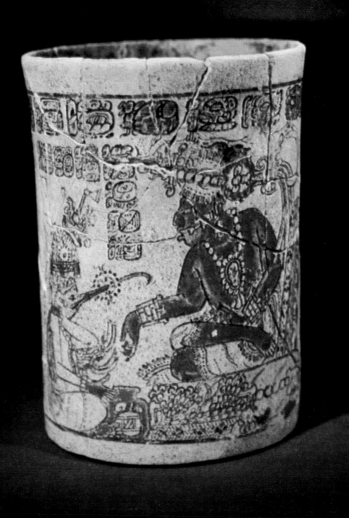

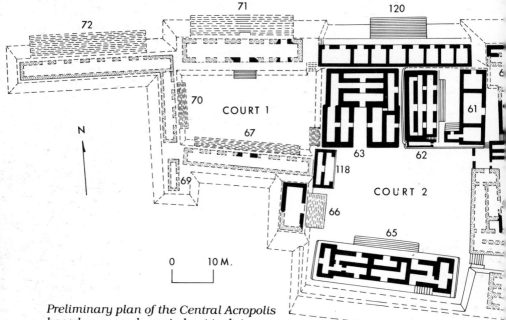

Preliminary plan of the Central Acropolis based upon work carried out to date.

Plaza Chultun

Well out in the Great Plaza and southeast of the stairway base of Temple II is the orifice of three connected subterranean chambers cut out of bedrock. The Maya term, *Chultun*, is applied to them. This chultun appears to have caved in centuries ago, thus exposing its opening. The diameter of the largest of the three chambers is about 7 $\frac{1}{2}$ feet, with a height of 4 feet. Over 280 bedrock features such as this have been recorded at Tikal. Many more lie hidden beneath plazas and the jungle floor. Some have been discovered in the Great Plaza in the course of excavation. These were sealed by Preclassic plaza floors. Archeologists are uncertain as to the original purpose of these chultuns though the possibility of food storage is suggested by recent experimental studies. Often they are found filled with trash, even human burials. However only a minor amount of debris was found within this particular chultun.

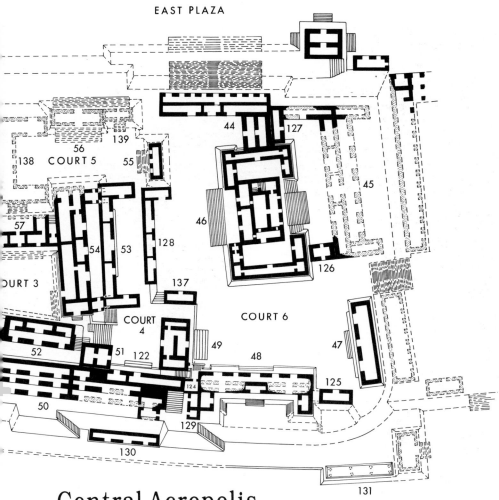

EAST PLAZA

44 127

56 139
138 COURT 5 55
45
57
46
54 53 128
126
DURT 3 137
COURT 6
COURT
4
49 47
52 51 122 48
124 125
50
129
130
131

Central Acropolis

On the south side of the Great Plaza and extending almost half the length of the East Plaza lies an immense complex composed of structures totally different from the temples just described. This complex, called the Central Acropolis, is almost 700 feet long, east to west, and covers about four acres. Although the Central Acropolis grew over the centuries in the same complicated fashion as the North Acropolis before reaching the final stage that is seen today, the result is totally different. In its latest stage it consists of six relatively small courts surrounded by long, low-lying buildings of one, two, or three stories, often containing many rooms. These buildings are termed "palaces" to distinguish them and their characteristics from the temples. However, the term "range-type buildings" is more objective than "palace" if one considers the many varieties of building plans which have been

Structure 5D-66 in Court 2 of the Central Acropolis.

Three identical stuccoed wooden figures of the Maya rain god found in Burial 195, A.D. 600. Height, 16 inches.

followed, and the degree of uncertainty as to what was the true function of the general building type.

As one walks through the Central Acropolis the levels of the various courts change in elevation, reflecting to some extent the natural fluctuations of the bedrock below. These courts are connected by intricate systems of stairways and passageways. The open spaces called courts are. the product of a combination of design and historical accident. In almost no case was the final form planned at the time of the earliest construction surviving in each court. Due to the gradual growth of the Acropolis and its eventual development of the court arrangement in the final phase, the palaces do not necessarily face onto a court, but may have their backs or sides turned onto one court while the actual façade looks onto another. The majority of these visible surface structures date to the Late Classic Period (A.D. 550-900).

Court 1

This court, already well above the level of the Great Plaza, has been left untouched. On three sides are the mounds of three separate low palaces which face into the court, while on the fourth or east side tower the walls of two buildings facing onto the adjacent and higher court.

Court 2

Access to the Central Acropolis is through Structure 5D-120, a multi-chambered building facing the south side of Temple I. Here in this second and highest court of the Acroplis, one encounters several of the best preserved palaces to be found in the entire complex. Two important points of interest relevant to the Acropolis in general are illustrated here. First, excavation has demonstrated that the court was not planned as such originally, but came into being through a process of addition, for the buildings surrounding it were constructed at different times. Secondly, while we refer to the low-lying nature of the palaces themselves, they were frequently built on top of high platforms, thus elevating them well above the surrounding terrain. This is the case with Structures 5D-58, 5D-61, 5D-62, and 5D-63 on the east and north boundaries of this court (see map). These buildings rest on platforms that extend about 16 feet below the level of the present court floor to an earlier buried floor at the same level as that of Court 1, to the west. Four of these structures existed before the court was raised, and all but one face to the east, away from the court itself. Bedrock is estimated to lie 30 to 50 feet below the present floor level, as the natural surface drops from north to south. Earlier constructions extending centuries back in time lie between bedrock and the final plaster floor of this court.

The court is dominated by the imposing and relatively late Structure 5D-65, or "Maler's Palace," rising two stories high on the south side. Here, Teobert Maler, the early explorer, lived during his explorations in Tikal, in 1895 and 1904. Immediately prior to the construction of

Maler's Palace, the court level was raised about 16 feet by the addition of an enormous mass of solid fill, thus providing a base upon which the palace could be built and, at the same time, burying the high supporting platforms of the eastern and northern palaces mentioned above. The lower story of Maler's Palace is composed of a series of rooms, arranged in two parallel ranges with additional rooms set at right-angles at the ends to form an "I" plan (see map). A carved frieze is visible above the three doorways facing the court, and a few remaining traces on other sides indicate that this frieze originally ran entirely around the palace, but is now preserved only on the north side. As in the temples, the doorways were without doors. The inner corners of the door jambs frequently have inset wooden dowels to which curtains could be attached from the inside. Just above the doorways and beneath the carved frieze on the exterior, one can also see a row of small holes that once held wooden dowels from which curtains may have been hung, or perhaps a canopy suspended over the court-side platform. Study has shown that various interior doorways were added, as were the second story, two exterior stairs, and all interior benches. Benches within the building were in some cases seats or even thrones for dignitaries, while in other cases they could have served as sleeping platforms. The interior wall plaster and wooden beams are original. Of particular interest are the graffiti, incised on the room walls, depicting ceremonial scenes and portraits. Although ranging in quality from crude to very fine, those found on the walls of Maler's Palace are among the most interesting at Tikal.

Across the court, north of Maler's Palace, stand three other palaces of Late Classic date. It was previously noted that three structures (5D-61, 5D-62, and 5D-63) are sustained by high platforms of earlier construction. By coincidence, their sequence of construction in time is in the same order as their present numeration, showing an expansion from east to west along the north side of the court. Structure 5D-61, now partially cleared and consolidated, faces east. It is a single-story palace containing three rooms, each with its own exterior doorway. A series of platform expansions at the rear of the building led to the eventual construction of 5D-62, the two stories of which also face east. Although the second story seems to have been incorporated in the original construction, it underwent some modification by the addition of the north room and the benches in the main room. The exterior stairway on the south end is integrated as a unit with the walls of the first story. Finally the westernmost of the three palaces, 5D-63, was constructed at a later date than 5D-62. The nine rooms of its single story, almost maze-like in plan, are arranged in the form of a "U." The partially restored remains of a number of small roof combs are visible on the flat roof. These are thought to have sustained carved decoration supplementing the frieze which is known to have existed around the entire upper zone of the palace walls. Unfortunately, this frieze is now lost, but the evidence of its presence in ancient times was found in the

Small pottery figurines made about A.D. 900.

Two-part pottery effigy of the Old God. A.D. 450. Height, 14 inches.

disintegrating carved stones which littered the bases of the palace walls. During its time of active use, Structure 5D-63 was also considerably altered by the sealing of old doorways and the opening of new ones, and by the addition of benches and windows.

The west side of the court is bounded by two very dissimilar buildings, Structures 5D-66, just north of Maler's Palace, and 5D-118, off the southwest corner of 5D-63. Almost temple-like with its single room perched on a small pyramid and reached by a long relatively wide stair, Structure 5D-66 raises many problems of function. In tunneling it and excavating the summit, no caches or burials were encountered, both fairly common features of buildings that functioned religiously. This one is not alone in the Central Acropolis in looking like a temple but lacking some of the usual signs of ceremonial usage. Structure 5D-66 was built at about the time of Maler's Palace and we can only guess that it functioned in connection with it, perhaps as a shrine. Structure 5D-118 is something else again. Jammed in the only remaining space, it is the latest building of this court. It is an especially peculiar building with its wide, almost open facade. The rear portion was definitely vaulted but the front chamber must have been either thatched or left unroofed.

For decades it has been undecided whether the "palaces" seen in this court were or were not residential and, despite extensive excavation throughout the Central Acropolis, this question persists. Various functional possibilities exist: temporary retreats or periodic residences of priests, permanent domiciles of ruling families, or purely administrative buildings populated by a white-collar class of adjudicators, scribes, and the like. If truly residential, where were the kitchens, and how was the debris of daily living disposed of? If purely administrative, the question arises why were so many "offices" required in Tikal? If the elite families of Tikal did not live here, where did they live? Some have queried whether these huge structures were really suitable for daily living, with their dampness, interior darkness, and such assumed inconveniences. But how damp were they when intact? In the context of the Maya culture were such considerations even important, or was it perhaps, much more important to occupy a house so imposing in aspect as to strike awe into the subjects or visitors who approached, heedless of the necessary discomforts required to achieve the effect? The whole manner in which the Acropolis grew by addition is suggestive of an expanding and extending family, or families, of great wealth and power. Furthermore, there is evidence in the nature of small added stairs, baffles, and sealed doorways, that an effort was made to maintain privacy when conditions of expansion began to threaten this commodity. Would such privacy be required if the buildings served a purely administrative or public function? And so the "palace" arguments go on and the visitor is invited to add his own specultions as to their functions. It is felt that the best explanation is one of duality of residence and administration. The feature of added second stories on so many

Interior of the Bat Palace showing the vulted arch and interconnecting rooms.

structures could represent an abandonment of nearly all rooms of the first story to administrative uses while the family moved upstairs. It is a fascinating problem.

Five-Story Palace

Directly east of the east end of Maler's Palace is the famed Late Classic "Five-Story Palace" (extensions of Structure 5D-58 intervene). This palace, extending down to the brink of the ravine where the Palace Reservoir is located (see below), consists of two parts: the upper three stories (Structure 5D-52 and the lower and later two stories (Structure 5D-50). With few exceptions, each story consists of two galleries, with the front gallery of the upper story set over the rear gallery of the range below, thus imparting a terraced effect to the five stories. A complicated series of exterior stairs led from one floor to another of the building itself, while two great stairways led from the lowest range down to a

Jade jaguar found in Burial 196, A.D. 700. Length 6 ¹/₂ inches.

Dancing figure of jade, 4 inches high. A.D. 450.
Stolen from Tikal Museum, September 1981.

terrace in the ravine below. These latter two stairways were built adjacent to a high, sloping stone wall which served as the south façade of the Acropolis. The earliest construction was the first story of the upper building, which was originally erected as a single-story palace and decorated by a deeply carved medial frieze now visible on the north and west sides. The second story was added next, together with its access stair at the east end. This was followed by construction of Structure 5D-51, a small two-room palace resting on a lower level to the immediate east of 5D-52. Finally, the lower ranges of Structure 5D-50 and probably the third story of 5D-52 were added at the same time. The sequence of these constructions, as determined by excavation, indicates that this entire series pre-dates the erection of Maler's Palace. Radiocarbon dates on the upper palace indicate an initial construction date of about A.D. 650. Of special note in the upper palace are the spindle-shaped vault beams in the rear gallery of the second story. The front gallery has almost totally collapsed.

Tunneling beneath the upper building of the Five-Story Palace revealed an Early Classic structure which had been razed to shoulder height by the Maya in preparation for the construction of the present building. A total depth of about 50 feet of construction lies below the upper building, extending back in time to the Preclassic Period.

Court 3

The buildings on the north and east sides of Court 3, behind or north of the Five-Story Palace, are believed to be contemporary with the first story of Structure 5D-52. In the vaults of the standing portions of these buildings can be seen the same spindle-shaped vault beams described in Structure 5D-52. The eastern building of this court (Structure 5D-54) actually faces east and in its final stage represented a complex of three broadly terraced stories. As it is the rear side of this palace which is seen from Court 3, a more detailed description is found below with Court 6.

Court 4

Moving still eastward, we encounter a very small rectangular court tucked away in the afternoon shadows of the towering Five-Story Palace. In this region, if one wished to move from the lowest range of 5D-50 to one of the northern courts, it was necessary to climb two flights of stairs and descend again at least one flight. This constant necessity to negotiate stairs reflects the complex multi-level composition of the Central Acropolis.

Structure 5D-49 on the east side of this small court consists of two parallel rooms on a north-south axis with a transverse room at each end. The building was accessible from both the east and west sides, but its principal orientation was to the east as indicated by a broad stair on

A reconstruction by H. Stanley Loten of Court 4, as seen from Structure 5D-46.

that side descending into the great eastern court of the Acropolis (Court 6). The south transverse room is almost intact and can convey to the visitor an impression of the appearance of the original interior. The stones employed in the construction of the walls of 5D-49 are unusual by virtue of being small, almost brick-sized on the exterior face. Only a small portion of a second story has survived the damage of time.

Across the court on the west side is a smaller two-room palace, which was constructed with similar masonry techniques. This small palace is numbered 5D-51 and retains some vestiges of the complicated and beautiful frieze which once adorned the east and north sides. An additional unusual feature which sets 5D-49 and 5D-51 apart from other palaces is the fact that there is no change in floor level between the rooms. Both of these relatively small buildings were constructed at a later date than the long, single-galleried palace, 5D-122, which stretches across the south side of the comfortably enclosed court. Although quite poorly preserved today, enough remains to show that Structure 5D-122 originally opened through doorways to the north. Above these doorways ran a carved frieze which included at least one large, grotesque mask, and very likely there were many others which have fallen.

One of the dominant features here is a pair of stairways sweeping upwards in the northwest corner of this court. The broadest (and earliest) of these stairs leads from Court 4 up to Court 3 behind the Five-Story Palace. The narrower stair is built partially over the "grand staircase" and leads to a room associated with Structure 5D-54 to the north of the Court.

Court 6

The largest of the Central Acropolis, this court is frequently referred to as the "great eastern court" since it maintains the largest open spaces as well as some of the most imposing constructions seen in the Acropolis.

Court 6 is entered by descending a stair from the north side of Court 4, whereupon one sees to the west the enormous height of the tiered palaces, Structures 5D-128, 5D-53, and, at the summit, the two-storied 5D-54. To the east we see the complex arrangement of Structure 5D-46. Although Court 6 is spacious and open, it is dominated by these out-sized palaces.

Structure 5D-53 rests on a broad terrace at the level of Court 4. This building comprises a single long gallery and, set at right angles to its extremities, two additional rooms. The first story of 5D-54, set above and slightly west of 5D-53, is more elaborate than 53. It also is somewhat earlier than 53 which was built at the time of adding the second story to 5D-54 (if this sounds complicated, remember that the Maya probably also had difficulty in describing what they were up to). The plan of the first story of 5D-54 is a variation of the common palace type, one with two parallel galleries with transverse rooms at each end. The basic plan of this structure, built fairly early in Late Classic times, underwent various changes through the addition of transverse walls breaking the long galleries into rooms. The routes of access between 5D-53 and the two stories of 5D-54 are something of a problem. It appears that the Maya allowed for no easy access between one building and another, but rather arranged matters so that each story had to be approached by roundabout routes from Courts 3, 4, and 5.

Below the terrace fronting 5D-53, we see at the level of Court 6, the palace known as 5D-128, made up of a series of rooms set in the familiar "U" pattern, reflecting the form and size of the earlier 5D-53 directly above and behind it. A small single-room building, referred to as 5D-137, probably formed in the Maya mind the south wing of 5D-128 despite the two being separated by a stairway leading down from Court 4 to Court 6.

Directly east of 5D-128 is Structure 5D-46, similarly resting at the level of Court 6. Viewed from the top story of 5D-54, to the west, this great palace, known prosaically as 5D-46, is seen in a way that reveals its extraordinary complex interior plan. The whole palace consists of a central Early Classic two-storied building with wings added to its north and south sides. The central building is one of two Early Classic

Head, 1 ¹/₂ inches high, of figurine of
jade and shell mosaic work. A.D. 450.

An intricately decorated pottery vessel recovered from an Early Classic cached offering set beneath the west stairway of Structure 5D-46.

palaces known to have survived in use to the end of Classic times. Since the entire unit is raised on a high platform, almost fortress-like, the central palace is reached by broad stairs on both its east and west sides. Trenching and tunneling beneath the west stairs yielded an elaborate cached offering of flint and shell objects as well as a beautifully carved vessel containing a figurine and many medallions of jade, shell, pyrite and obsidian mosaic work. Four Late Classic burials were recovered from beneath a series of superimposed stairs on the east side of 5D-46.

The palace itself possesses two stories connected by a twisting interior staircase, the only one known from Tikal. Adjacent to the north and south ends of the central building are major Late Classic additions consisting of small open-air patios surrounded by rooms on their three sides. From the north patio a spectacular example of Maya art in stone and thin plaster can be viewed. Fashioned in Late Classic times and revealed in 1965 by excavation, this is the best preserved decorative frieze in the Central Acropolis. It belongs to Structure 5D-44, the "L"-shaped palace immediately north of 5D-46. This frieze was preserved by having been covered by the north room of the north patio of 5D-46. This phenomenon of intruding and abutting new architectural features not only allows the archaeologist to establish the sequence of construction but on occasion, notably this, reveals to us by pure accident the wealth of ornamentation lavished on these buildings by the Maya.

A seeming maze of Late Classic constructions just east of 5D-46 has created a small and very private court which could be entered only by passing through one of the surrounding palaces. It was from this very restricted court that the main access to the Early Classic portion of 5D-46 was maintained during Late Classic times. The buildings about this small court include 5D-45, 5D-126, and 5D-127. By A.D. 800 or 900, access in such areas as this had become so restricted that an intimate knowledge of these compounds was necessary to traverse successfully the Acropolis from one end to the other.

Directly south of 5D-46 lies another "U"-shaped structure, 5D-48, overlooking the huge ravine or "Palace Reservoir." Its most open side, facing the ravine, comprises a private enclosed patio. This Late Classic palace was built originally with two galleries, but onto this were later added side wings which provide the final "U" shape. Other buildings which abut the ends of 5D-48 are still later additions.

Court 5

Northwest of Structure 5D-54 the visitor enters the largely unexcavated Court 5. This area closes the circuit about the Central Acropolis. Here, still-buried Late Classic rooms once towered to a height of three stories to the west and south sides, while low structures bounded the north side. This court has been left almost untouched in order to illustrate how the Central Acropolis appeared before trowels, picks, and shovels exposed what lay beneath the great mounds and slopes. The contrast is vivid between this court and Court 6. Much of Tikal's past splendour lies as buried and mute as the architectural wealth that can be barely guessed beneath the hills of debris forming "Court 5."

It has been estimated that the visible final stage of the Central Acropolis, an incomparable architectural achievement in ancient America, incorporated 42 individual structures, with some five hundred years of building activity in this final stage alone, while centuries of construction underlie this prodigious achievement. An extensive program of consolidation and restricted restoration has been conducted throughout the Central Acropolis in order to preserve and present to the visitor the unique grandeur of this, only one complex portion of Tikal. The very essence of Classic Maya civilization is contained both here in the Central Acropolis and, to the north, in the Great Plaza and the North Acropolis. It was here, the clear center of Tikal, that both gods and men were manipulated over centuries in ways and for ends that scholars may never fully understand.

Palace Reservoir

The Central Acropolis rests on the north edge of a deep ravine called the "Palace Reservoir." Investigation has shown that, while water was deliberately drained toward the ravine and collected in the eastern end of it, the quantity involved was rather small in relation to the great size of the ravine itself. The entire south face of the Central Acropolis was walled for the greater portion of its visible height. At the foot of this wall was a terrace upon which buildings had been constructed (including a possible kitchen, Structure 5D-131), and evidence indicates that the level of water maintained in the reservoir never rose as high as this terrace. What appears to be a dike blocks the east end of this great depression. Although this "dike" serves as an eastern boundary for the small reservoir, it also conveniently serves as a causeway or road providing access between the many groups of buildings that lie on both sides of the ravine. It is conceivable that the ravine itself was used as a quarry from which much of the material was obtained for construction in the Central Acropolis and other surrounding features. Future expanded excavation and study are required to determine the exact amount of water maintained in this reservoir, although it is already evident that it was sufficient to supply the needs of the Central Acropolis if the latter were indeed residential.

East Plaza

The East Plaza, north of the east portion of the Central Acropolis and east of the Great Plaza, was once a great formal area, 5 $1/2$ acres in size, plastered throughout. A number of buildings of great interest are located here. Both the Méndez and Maler Causeways enter the plaza. Those who arrive from the southeast via the Méndez Causeway pass a large temple on their left, Structure 5D-38, at the top of the ascent of the Causeway. This imposing temple, facing west, is Late Classic in date and features a small masonry one-roomed shrine on its stairway. Only the upper portions of the vaults of the temple rooms are visible beneath the massive, partially fallen roof comb. An excavation in 1964 at the base of the stairway uncovered a cache of severed human heads, a sure sign of human sacrifice.

Directly north of this temple is the colossal rectangular Platform 5E-1, measuring almost 380 feet by 400 feet as its base and standing some 25 above the East Plaza. Despite quite considerable excavation, the nature of this feature and its function remain one of the major puzzles of Tikal archaeology. Several walls and a huge mask of a Classic construction were found well buried near the southwest basal corner of the platform. However, excavations on the top of the platform revealed nothing but incomplete mounds of rubble fill. It is possible that whatever palaces, floors, temples, or even monuments were once covering this great platform were at some time completely removed. It is also conceivable that an enlargement of earlier construction was begun and never finished. Very late construction has been found at the base of the platform, including a long, multi-doorway building along the entire west base.

Close to the center of the east base of this same platform are the remains of the only known sweatbath at Tikal, Structure 5E-22, in the large plaza of "Group F" (containing, among other buildings, Structure 5E-1). Built in Late Classic times, this fascinating building features a low doorway on its east side (to prevent the escape of vapor), a narrow channel leading north which was flanked by broad raised benches, and a round firepit at the center of the rear wall. It is here that the Maya took purifying steam baths on ritual occasions and, on others, probably to cure their ills. Therapeutic sweating has been found in highland Guatemala today. How many other buildings with this function occur at Tikal is unknown. This is the only one to have been restored and to have been recognized as such.

In the center of the East Plaza and just west of Platform 5E-1 lies the so-called "Market Place." This consists of a quadrangular arrangement of long low buildings (Structures 5E-32 through 36). The outer perimeter of buildings, measuring 200 by 280 feet, comprises four double-range buildings attached at their corners, with multi-doorwayed rooms looking both into the compound and out onto the Plaza. Entry to the inner rectangularly arranged four buildings (which are essentially like the outer ones in plan and construction) was via passageways and stairs through and over the outer buildings. No benches, curtain holders, or other feastures of the Central Acropolis palaces were found in these Late Classic East Plaza ranges. They appear to have been used differently than the long palace-like buildings seen in the Central Acropolis. The most likely explanation for this great complex is that it served as a public market. Its location would have been ideal for such a center.

To the west, between the "Market Place" and the rear of Temple I is the East Plaza ballcourt. The playing court lay between the two structures and, interestingly, had a profile of benches and aprons unlike that of the courts south of Temple I and in the "Plaza of the Seven Temples." The East Plaza court appears to have been built very late in Classic times. Each structure carries along its top a building facing into the court, with a façade made up of columns fashioned from radially set masonry blocks. Running along each side of the court was an elaborately carved frieze of hieroglyphs, Following the collapse of Tikal around A.D. 900, people continued to be interested in the court, as is evidenced by masonry blocking walls, trash, and other construction from early Postclassic times.

Just south of the ballcourt is the remarkable Structure 5D-43. This apparent temple was built against the northeast corner of the Central Acropolis and, in some manner, probably functioned in connection with the ballgame. It was built in Late Classic times. Now consolidated and partially restored, it consists of a large platform served by three stairways and it supports a two-room building with all but the north, or principal, doorway blocked by Maya masonry. The fascinating feature of this structure is the platform with its complex sloping, projecting, and inset moldings and enclosed decorative elements. The whole effect is very Mexican and reminiscent of architecture at the great site of Teotihuacán and its successor, Tula, all in the vicinity of Mexico City. Two other comparable platforms (Structures 6E-144 and 5C-53) have been excavated at Tikal with essentially the same decorative composition seen on 5D-43.

West Plaza

The rarely visited West Plaza, west and north of Temple II, has undergone considerable excavation by the Tikal Project. A high, large Late Classic palace (Structure 5D-15) occupies much of the north side of the Plaza. This palace overlies a complicated sequence of earlier construction. Of particular interest is the relatively small mound on the west side of the Plaza. This structure, 5D-11, is another example of unfinished construction, undertaken at about the end of Classic times. While it was evidently intended to be a temple, excavators could find no trace of a stairway, nor of room walls and floor, let alone finished masonry on the flanks. Yet deep underneath it was a fine tomb, Burial 77, replete with beautiful Late Classic pottery. A single adult extended

Of light green jade, this Late Classic pendant, 3 $^1/_2$ inches high, is one of the loveliest known from the Maya area. It is from Burial 77. Stolen from Tikal Museum. 1981.

on the floor, wearing one of the loveliest jade pendants ever found in Maya archaeology, and a roof of logs covered by a woven mat over which had been sprinkled thousands of pieces of obsidian and flint. Something, as yet unexplained, intervened to halt the completion of this important Late Classic building.

Throughout the West Plaza are many tumbled stelae and altars. Those close to the features just described are all Late Classic. The Early Classic carved Stela 15, however, occurs with them. Excavation indicates that all of these monuments probably owe their final and discovered positions to the efforts of Postclassic peoples. This is certainly true for Stela 15. The large plain monuments may be lying where they were suddenly abandoned by the very late Classic Maya.

We have now described the true center of Tikal, consisting of the East and West Plazas, the Central Acropolis, the North Acropolis, and the Great Plaza with its opposed Temples I and II. Immense as all of this is, the map of Tikal shows how diminutive it is in relation to the site as a whole. But the amount of construction that ocurred here, where every level is artificial and centuries of effort underlie practically every feature one stands on, cannot be compared with anything else in ancient America. The monuments of Copán are far more beautiful than those at Tikal, the palaces of Palenque perhaps more graceful and open, but no other site matches the depth, height, and intricacy of evolution and productivity of Tikal, particularly at its center.

Head of a god resting in a plate, carved on the side of Altar 6.

75

The lintel of Temple III, best seen in early morning light.

Temple III

The road running through the Great Plaza continues west to Temple IV. At the southwest corner of the West Plaza it passes the tree-covered flanks of Temple III, known as the Temple of the Jaguar Priest, after the scene portrayed on a lintel within its rooms. Temple III stands about 180 feet high and has two instead of three tandemly placed temple rooms (as in Temples I, II, and IV). Temple III was built in Late Classic times. A construction date of 9.19.0.0.0, or A.D. 810, is suggested by one reading of the fragmentary text of Stela 24 at the base of its stairway. Altar 6 occurs with the stela and though it is damaged and incomplete, the visitor can clearly make out on its side a grotesque head of a deity resting in a plate with three feet. A woven mat, the symbol of authority, is carved on either side. The text of the altar, carved on top around the edge, is eroded. It has been impossible to restore the carved stela to its original condition, as many fragments are missing. It is suspected that

Postclassic peoples tampered with the shattered stela, or may even have broken it themselves.

The stair and rooms of Temple III face east. Access is difficult but worth the effort. The outer doorway and lintel have been restored. The inner doorway is spanned by an almost intact carved lintel depicting a grotesquely obese central personage, completely clothed in jaguar skin except for hands, feet, and face which are bare. He is flanked by two individuals holding staves and what appear to be three-pronged eccentric flints. This lintel and Lintel 2 in Temple I are the only ones of the seven known at Tikal to have survived in position.

Just south of Temple III, across the road, is a small mound excavated in 1964. It yielded a Late Classic one-room shrine, once vaulted, oriented east and associated with piles of pottery and smashed incense burners of Postclassic peoples who were still using its facilities for their ceremonies.

Bat Palace

The road bends around the rear of Temple III. Here, one can look up and see the back of the soaring roof comb with a mask panel in its center. A few hundred feet beyond, on the left, is a huge palace compound, one structure of which (5C-13) is consolidated. The "Bat Palace," as it is known, consists of a double-range lower story and a single-range upper story, the latter now consolidated. In ground plan it resembles the letter "I" in much the same way as Maler's Palace in the central Acropolis. The vaults of the Bat Palace are stepped. Numerous graffiti and benches occur throughout the interconnecting ranges of rooms. Low windows look west from the back rooms. The whole quadrangle probably belongs to Late Classic times. Without excavation, what underlies it is still unknown.

Twin-pyramid Complex N

Between the Bat Palace and Temple IV the road runs through what is referred to as a "Twin-pyramid Complex." Seven of these are known at Tikal and are features unique to this site. This group is known as Complex N to distinguish it from the others. It was built at 9.14.0.0.0, or A.D. 711, a date established by Stela 16 in this group. A Twin-pyramid Complex is made up of two essentially identical pyramids, one to the east, the other to the west, with a plaza in between. Neither pyramid has any trace of a building on top. Both are rectangular in plan with a stairway on each side, four in all. The west base of the east pyramid faces a row of west-oriented stelae and paired altars, always plain. At the north center of the plaza stands an "enclosure," facing south with a single doorway but no substructure or roof of any type. The doorway was vaulted. In the open interior are a stela and altar, which are carved in most cases. On the south side of the plaza, to complete the pattern, is a low, relatively small, palace-type building, in all known cases having nine doorways, the whole facing north. A group such as this was erected at 20-year intervals —the Maya *Katun*— throughout much of Late Classic times at Tikal. As noted, this particular group was built at 9.14.0.0.0, marking the 14th Katun of the 9th Baktun (a Baktun being a cycle of 400 Maya years; see Appendix). As time went on, the south palace underwent numerous modifications, for what reason is not known. The purpose of such groups as a whole is still a question. Like so many features at Tikal, they can be described as to composition, development, dating, etc., but how they really functioned is always difficult and frequently impossible to say with anything more than outright speculation.

The carved monuments in the north enclosure of Complex N, Stela 16 and Altar 5, are among the finest at Tikal. Stela 16 has text and scene carved on the front (rarely were the sides carved in Late Classic times and never the rear). The text is abbreviated as to dedicatory date, merely noting completion of a Katun 14 (note two bars with a value of 5 each and four dots worth four, or 14 in all, in the upper glyph panel) of an implied Baktun 9. The altar top consists of a circumferential band of beautiful hieroglyphs and a central scene of two elaborately garbed priests standing behind an altar on which a human cranium and a group of thigh bones rest.

Altar 5, with a diameter of 5 1/2 feet, depicts two elaborately garbed persons conferring behind an altar piled with human femurs and a skull.

*Stela 16 can be studied by the hour for the
wealth of Late Classic costuming to be seen on it.*

Tozzer Causeway

On leaving this Twin-pyramid Complex, the road turns sharply left and enters the Tozzer Causeway (running east to the West Plaza) which here rises sharply towards the massive basal platform supporting the greatest structure of all, the Late Classic Temple IV, or the Temple of the Double-headed Serpent (its lintel motif).

Temple IV

Temple IV, facing east, stands 212 feet from the base of the platform supporting its pyramid to the top of its roof comb, the highest standing aboriginal New World structure. (There are good grounds for believing that the Pyramid of the Sun at Teotihuacán, northeast of Mexico City, originally was slighly higher, since nothing is left of the temple that stood on its summit). The point is that Temple IV stands higher than any other building known in Precolumbian America, especially if one includes the elevation of its basal platform. The breadth of the building and its pyramid belie the height of Temple IV. It is estimated that some 250,000 cubic yards of construction material have been incorporated in Temple IV and its supporting platform. The area about the temple is pockmarked by quarries. Still to be determined is whether Temple IV overlies an earlier version of what one sees today.

The now ruined stairway of the basal platform provides access to the pyramid proper. At the center of the base of the pyramid stairway are a plain stela and its altar. One climbs the pyramid at its northeast corner, up and over the root-entangled terraces. It is a difficult climb but well worth it. The recently consolidated and partially restored temple is made up of three rooms, with walls up to 40 feet thick. The temple proper rests on a building platform, itself built on what is called a supplementary platform which sits directly on the top of the pyramid. The plan of the temple is identical with such other roughly contemporary great Tikal temples as I and II in the use of step-downs from front to rear, side indentations, and, at the rear, a narrow, vertical projection. Standing beneath the plain outer lintel and looking east one can see the nearest great temple, number III, its roof comb rising above the forest, with Temples II and I beyond it. The great mass on the skyline to the southeast is the South Acropolis. The summit of the roof comb of Temple V, the fifth of the great temples, can be seen just beyond the South Acropolis. The topography about Tikal is best appreciated from the vantage point of Temple IV. A metal ladder on the south side of the building allows one to climb still higher to the roof and the base of the enormous roof comb.

The middle and inner doorways were once spanned by beautifully carved lintels, both now in the museum in Basel, Switzerland (an epoxy cast of the innermost lintel is exhibited in the National Museum

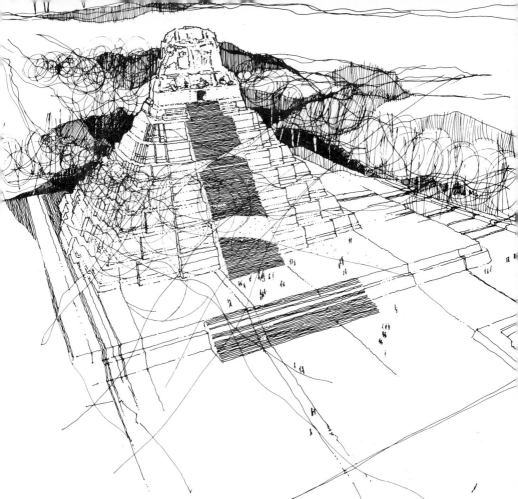

Temple IV, the greatest of the Tikal religious buildings.
A reconstruction by Wilbur Pearson based upon his detailed architectural drawings.

of Archaeology and Ethnology, Guatemala City). The impressions of the once-concealed tops of the individual beams of the lintel are preserved above the doorways. The lintels apparently were carved elsewhere, then laboriously transported up to the temple rooms (*zapote* wood weighs about 70 pounds per cubic foot) and installed on the wall-top bed prepared for them. They were wrapped in woven mats, well bound to protect them from dripping plaster. The vaults were built next, then the roof, and finally the roof comb. When all was secure, the exposed matting was cut away, leaving the buried portion on top of each lintel to rot away. The hieroglyphic inscriptions on these lintels indicate that the temple was built at about 9.15.10.0.0, or A.D. 741 in the usually accepted Maya-Christian correlation (see Appendix). A long series of radiocarbon dates on lintel beams and vault beams give an average age of A.D. 720 ± 60, which helps to confirm the correlation.

81

Maudslay Causeway

From Temple IV one can proceed to the relatively isolated North Zone or Group H via the Maudslay Causeway. This begins off the northeast corner of the building platform of Temple IV. Both the causeway and the North Zone were not discovered until 1937. As are all five of the Tikal Causeways, this is a raised road, flanked by parapets or walls with intermittent exits. The Maudslay Causeway ranges from about 130 to 190 feet wide and originally was paved the whole way with plaster. It runs a distance of about a half a mile. A narrow jungle road, follows it now.

Group H and Twin-pyramid Complex P

Running in a northeasterly direction from Temple IV, the Maudslay Causeway terminates at a large plaza bordered on the north and east sides by Late Classic temples, Structures 3D-40 through 43, as well as Twin-pyramid Complex P. The whole area was called "Group H" by Morley and is designated as the "North Zone" on the map of Tikal. The excavated and partially restored temples were probably built around A.D. 700 to judge from the types of masonry employed. The huge platform sustaining the twin north-oriented diminutive Structures 3D-41 and 42, and the massive 43, very likely overlies a good deal of prior architecture. Structure 3D-43 has all the characteristics of a temple except that it has no roof comb. Its three interior rooms are as large as any known elsewhere at Tikal. The graffiti upon its room walls are especially interesting. Acres of great and small, totally ruined and still untouched buildings surround these temples.

Twin-pyramid Complex P, just west of this great platform, is typical of these groups in all respects. The carved Stela 20 and its beautiful Altar 8 stand in the north enclosure. The stela was erected at 9.16.0.0.0, or A.D. 751. The final version of the Maudslay Causeway is thought to have been built to connect Temple IV and this group at about this time.

Twin-pyramid Complex M

An earlier Twin-pyramid Complex, built at 9.13.0.0.0, and a short distance southwest of this one, appears to have been abandoned at the time of building the causeway. This group is known as Twin-pyramid Complex M and comprises Structures 3D-98 through 100 and various monuments. The Maya practically leveled the west pyramid (98). Three plain stelae survive in front of the east pyramid (100) while the largely demolished enclosure to the north, Structure 3D-99, still contains Altar 14 and Stela 30 (A.D. 692). The altar exhibits on its top an outsized Ahau glyph with the attached number 8, and about it is the circular inscription that records the Long Count date 9.13.0.0.0,

Altar 8, with prostrate figure, a typical theme throughout much of the span of Tikal monumental art.

one which correlates with the day 8 Ahau (see Appendix, Short Count). The stela (reconstructed and re-erected) shows a standing priest with a ceremonial bar, facing left, and is most unusual in completely lacking an inscription. The south palace no longer exists, having been torn out to make way for the causeway. Materials gained from this group probably contributed to the construction of the causeway. As with monuments and temples, as we have shown, nothing tangible was conceived of by the Maya as permanent. This Twin-pyramid Complex had served its usefulness —whatever that may have been— and it stood in the way of something new, so it was partially dismantled and by-passed.

Group H or the North Zone and the incredible number of palace compounds and temple clusters throughout it form still another incalculably rich problem for excavation. However, it is one that will require a great deal of time and money to do properly.

*Drawing of rock sculpture along the course of the
Maler Causeway by Antonio Tejada*

Maler Causeway

If Group H is visited by vehicle, one has to retrace one's route to Temple IV. But if on foot, the visitor can turn south from the plaza in front of the great temple platform and descend the great incline of the Maler Causeway. Narrower than the Maudslay Causeway, this road runs straight south to the East Plaza behind Temple I, a distance of about two-fifths of a mile. It is flanked by easily visible parapets, now collapsed. Close to the bottom of the descent from the elevated North Zone, the trail along the causeway passes by a large rectangular outcrop of limestone bedrock. This was carved in Late Classic times with two life-sized individuals, nearly naked, with bound limbs as if captives (a common motif at Tikal on many monuments, both early and late). The scene measures close to 12 by 20 feet.

Twin-pyramid Complexes Q, R, O

Midway along the causeway after a steep climb one enters a zone of considerable construction. Extending east-west almost one-third of a mile are three Twin-pyramid Complexes, lettered respectively Q, R, and O from east to west. The central one, R, closest to the causeway, has been left essentially as found after test excavations. All the elements of these complexes are present here (east and west pyramid, for example). Stela 19 and Altar 6 stand restored in the enclosure. The stela dates to 9.18.0.0.0, or A.D. 790. This is the latest of this

Perspective drawing by Norman Johnson of
the Twin-pyramid Complex erected in A.D. 771.

type of group found at Tikal. Of interest is the fact that one of the plain stelae in front of the east pyramid is missing. The altar once with it lies way out of place next to the automobile road. Excavation indicates that Postclassic peoples were probably responsible for removing the stela, for their own purposes. The altar (P52) was simply abandoned by them where it is found today.

The westernmost group, Twin-pyramid Complex O, differs only in size from others. One pecualiarity, however, is the plain stela and altar, rather than carved ones, in the north enclosure. Study suggests that this group was constructed at 9.15.0.0.0, or A.D. 731. This group is reached by a trail running west from the causeway.

The east complex, the largest of all and lettered Q (commonly designated as Group E, a holdover from Morley's system), occupies a raised platform covering an area of over 5 acres. It is here that the composition of these special groups can best be appreciated, for the monuments have been re-erected, and the east pyramid, south palace, and north enclosure have been largely restored. Stela 22 and Altar 10, discovered in 1956, are within the enclosure and are superb examples of Late Classic Tikal sculpture. They were carved and erected in 9.17.0.0.0 or A.D. 771. As in so many cases of monuments not destroyed by the Classic Maya, the visitor will note the mutilated face of the sculptured personage on the stela. Even the face on a garter has been intentionally mutilated. One can only guess that this was done

85

Upper portion of the hieroglyphic text of Stela 22 in which its date is given.

by Postclassic peoples who thought that by doing so they would somehow weaken the lingering power of the stela or of the person depicted on it. The carved hand appears to be scattering either water or corn. The inscription on this stela occurs in two vertical separated panels. The date is inscribed in the first four glyphs of the upper panel, in the upper two rows. The first glyph records the day 13 Ahau, followed by the month 18 Cumku; the left hand glyph in the second row is the Katun glyph surmounted by the number 17, or 17th Katun, while the second glyph, to the right in this row, records that the Haab, or Tun, is completed. These four glyphs state that a day in a 52-year cycle, 13 Ahau 18 Cumku, completes Katun 17 of an implied Baktun 9; in other words, 9.17.0.0.0 (see Appendix). A bound individual, presumably a captive, decorates the unfortunately eroded top of the altar. The carved periphery shows seated roped individuals with interspaced mat designs.

Twin-pyramid Complex L

While on the subject of Twin-pyramid Complexes, it should be noted that a seventh exists, lettered L, south of Temple IV in a fairly inaccessible spot. It was almost totally demolished in ancient times, and archaeologists suspect that this was done to provide fill for the construction of Temple IV, around A.D. 740. Only fallen plain monuments survive on the surface. The enclosure, now totally gone, contains a plain stela and altar (Stela P41 and Altar P43). A probable date of construction is 9.12.0.0.0 (or A.D. 672), based on the pattern of Katuns, or 20-Maya-year intervals in the building of these enigmatic groups.

Mendez Causeway

Other areas of Tikal are easily reached by the visitor. Two well marked routes, for instance, lead to the famed Temple of the Inscriptions, almost a mile south of the Jungle Inn and another mile southeast of the Great Plaza, via the Méndez Causeway. With a length of about three-fifths of a mile and an average width of 200 feet, this causeway originates at the east side of the East Plaza (behind Temple I), passing by Group G, and runs almost straight to the Temple of the Inscriptions. Close to the East Plaza the Late Classic causeway with its parapets overlies an earlier causeway without side parapets. The latter may be Early Classic.

Temple of the Inscriptions

The Temple of the Inscriptions is aptly named (though technically it is known as Structure 6F-27). The central portion of the rear of the 40-foot high roof comb, somewhat less than the height of the building and pyramid combined, is covered with hieroglyphs to form a text comparable to those on monuments. Panels of glyphs occur on the sides of the roof comb as well and on the cornice. This huge inscription records the date 9.16.15.0.0 (A.D. 766). This temple was discovered as recently as 1951 and was first reported by Antonio Ortiz, of today's Jungle Inn. Facing west, the two-room temple dominates a large walled-in plaza. At the base of the temple stairway are Stela 21 and Altar 9. Both stela and altar have been repaired and the stela re-erected. However, large portions of the latter are missing. A metate, used for grinding corn, was found in an area populated 50-75 years ago by people from Lake Petén-Itzá. It was obvious that the metate had been made from a fragment of a carved stela: it fit Stela 21, some two-fifths of a mile southeast of where the metate was found. This well illlustrates how much disturbance has occurred at Tikal. Stela 21 was once a magnificent monument; the remaining text, enviably carved and

A panel of beautifully carved hieroglyphs, 22 inches high. Stela 20.

preserved, at the left base of the front, is sufficient to give its date, 9.15.5.0.0, or A.D. 736. The altar has carved on its top a large bound captive, lying on his stomach. As noted, this is a very frequent motif at Tikal.

Plaza of the Seven Temples

Almost endless ruins are to be found south of the Central Acropolis and Temple III, across the Palace Reservoir. This is the location of the Plaza of the Seven Temples, the staggering mass of the South Acropolis, and many other pyramids, temples, and palaces, many of them with still standing masonry, and even intact rooms. There are three routes which lead to this area. One trail begins at the head of the Méndez Causeway and passes south by the temple with the stairway shrine (Structure 5E-38) and across the supposed dike at the east end of the Palace Reservoir. Another trail begins close to Temple II and leads to the South Acropolis via high terrain between the Palace and Temple Reservoirs. The third trail starts south of Temple III and is the most direct route to the Plaza of the Seven Temples.

Palace at South end of the Plaza of the Seven Temples Str. 5D-91.

The seven closely adjacent small Late Classic temples set in a row provide the name for this large plaza whose history goes back centuries before Christ. The restored central temple, Structure 5D-96, is the largest, and is fronted by a plain Late Classic stela and its altar. This temple is particularly intriguing for the medial molding heavily embellished with crossed bones, a skull, and other devices. Along the south side of the plaza are three Late Classic palaces (Structures 5D-90, 91, 92), the central one with a long gallery divided into rooms by walls that were later additions. Each corner of the upper façade is decorated by a projecting human head, still partially visible from below. In the upper part are to be seen several decorative elements resembling small, roof combs. The west side of the plaza is bounded by temple features evidently oriented toward the next plaza to the west. Two unexcavated west-oriented temples along the west side of the plaza are still fairly intact.

Triple Ballcourt

A triple ballcourt, made up of Structures 5D-78 through 81, occupies the north side of the plaza. These are larger versions of the court immediately south of Temple I. The three courts are essentially identical. Originally, in early Late Classic times, there was simply a single court here but later additions provided three parallel courts. The central court was rebuilt three times, while the outer courts went through two stages.

The plaza itself is the end product of a long history of construction. Excavations have shown that a long series of superimposed plaza floors once existed here, the earliest ones going back into Preclassic times. This confirms the opinion that Tikal was impressively large during very early times.

Lost World

A trail which branches to the west north of the ballcourts leads to the "Lost World" complex. Its principal structure is the Great Pyramid (5C-54). Standing close to 100 feet high it is square in plan with a stairway on each side. The most important is the stairway facing west which is flanked by terraces and gigantic masks, employing masonry blocks over six feet long. This pyramid is Late Preclassic in date and was one of the greatest structures of its time in all of Mesoamerica. Some 110 feet directly west of it is a low platform (5C-53). Excavated in 1964 it is a four-stairway rectangular platform with no trace of a building on top. The use of moldings along the sides and other details suggest that it was inspired by the architecture of Teotihuacán. It was built in early Late Classic times, around A.D. 600 and is a larger version of a tiny four-stairwayed platform found in the south part of Tikal and labeled on the map Str. 6E-144.

The Plaza opens out around these two structures to reveal two well-defined areas. To the south of the Great Pyramid are structures 6C-24 and 25. To the east we find Structure 5D-84 with its three chambers in a row; 5D-85 a two-part platform with access to the Plaza of the Seven Temples; 5D-86 a Late Classic structure has masks in its facade, Stela 39 was found here; 5D-87 sometimes known as the Temple of the Skulls is the third largest in the Lost World; and 5D-88 and 5D-89. To the north we find Structures 5D-77, 5C-45 and 46 plus a few lesser ones. The second area west of the Great Pyramid lies at a lower level and is now known as the "Low Plaza" of the Lost World. In the center is Structure 5C-53 mentioned above. To the north is Structure 5C-49. This is the second in importance in this area and is known as the Temple of Talud Tablero or Panel and Slope. Three different periods of construction one atop the other are evident in this structure. All three phases are visible at the lower southwest corner which was left uncovered during the restoration for the benefit of visitors. The Lost

LOST WORLD COMPLEX

or

(Great Pyramid Plaza)

N

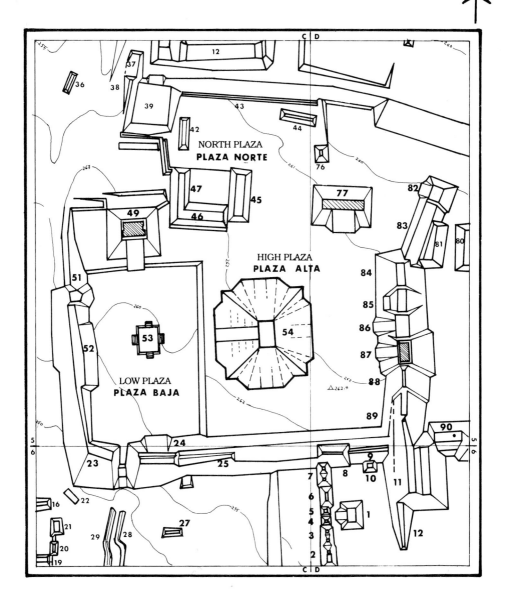

10 0   50 m.

World and its monuments were excavated, and restored by the National Tikal Park Project between 1979 and 1985.

Group 6C XVI

About 300 meters to the south of the Plaza, a trail leads to a "residential" area Known as 6C XVI. It is composed of various small plazas and structures with masks and murals on the walls. Excavation in the North Plaza of this complex revealed in Cache 049 a ballcourt marker considered one of the most extraordinary of its kind in Tikal. Made out of limestone, it bears several hieroglyphic texts beautifully carved. The marker is on exhibit at the National Museum in Guatemala City.

South Acropolis

The South Acropolis remains untouched by excavation. The top floor of this colossal rectangular mass of solid construction lies about 80 feet above the surrounding area; its square base covers close to five acres. The South Acropolis is difficult to climb, but on top of it are large, very early Late Classic palaces arranged about a central temple looking north (Structure 5D-104). In all likelihood, a complete sequence of architectural development lies within this mass, with beginnings far back in Preclassic times. Many years of trenching and tunneling would be required to Study its composition and growth.

Temple V

Temple V, one of the great temples of Tikal, stands looking north, just to the east of the South Acropolis. Radiocarbon tests indicate a construction date of about A.D. 700. Outstanding features include the rounded corners on the temple and its substructure and the raised edges of moldings on the sides of the great stairway. Excavation revealed no traces of monuments at the base of the stairway. Temple V stands close to 190 feet high and is unusual for the tiny single room at the top. This room had a breadth of only 21/2 feet, yet the rear wall is about 15 feet thick. Perhaps never was so much built to provide so little floor space. A large hole dug in the roof before our time provides accidental access to a series of superimposed roof comb chambers.

Access to the top of the roof comb by means of wooden ladders which was permitted, has now been forbidden as a conservation measure. Temple V has not been restored.

Other temples and palaces with intact features abound in this south area, frequently off the well marked trails, It is advisable not to wander, however, losing sight of trails, as the jungle provides few landmarks. It is quite possible to walk in a complete circle without knowing it.

Lost World Complex, Structure 5C-49, built during the Early Classic period. It is in the Teotihuacan style

Group F

Two other easily accessible groups remain to be described. Morley called one of them "Group F." A trail leads west from about the midpoint of the road leading from the Inn to its juncture with the Méndez Causeway. Group F consists of four enormous palace-type buildings (Structures 5E-1 and 4E-45, 47, and 48) arranged about a court. The whole complex occupies an area of about two acres. What one sees was built in Late Classic times. It has been partly consolidated.

Group G

Morley's "Group G" is just south of the juncture of the main road and the Méndez Causeway. This Group forms one of the largest clusters of major palace-type construction known at Tikal. The visitor can enter the first court through an enormous Late Classic palace reached directly by the trail. One feature of this multi-roomed structure is a vaulted interior passageway leading from the rear exterior of the building to the inner court in front of the building The entry to this tunnel is through the mouth of a huge monster mask. This palace consists of 29 vaulted chambers situated in the shape of a rectangular Ubearing vestiges of two other chambers in its northern and southern ends, forming a second story. This palace complex has been cleared and restored by the project sponsored bythe Guatemalan Government.

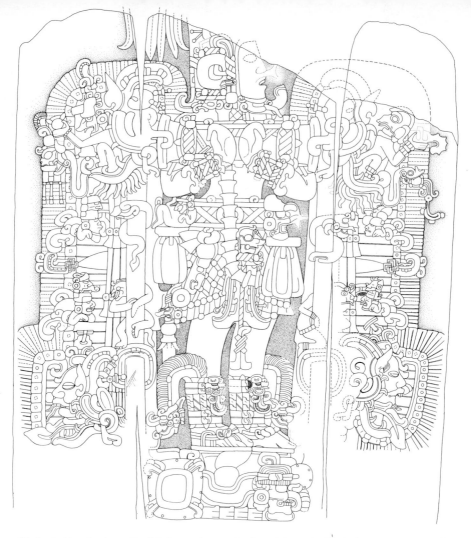

Stela 1, the design of which carries on to the sides. Included are a welter of figures climbing poles as well as heads and seated gods in the jaws of snakes.

THE CARVED MONUMENTS

Only a group of small carved monument fragments attest to the presence of major art in stone during Preclassic times. However, it is Stela 29, now exhibited in the Tikal Museum, that represents the earliest discovered use of hieroglyphic texts on a Tikal monument. Stela 29 is incomplete. The lower half was missing when the stela was found in what apparently was an ancient dump, well north of Temple III. This, the earliest-known inscribed lowland Maya monument, was most probably carved in A.D. 292. The latest-known Tikal stela is number 11, in the Great Plaza, carved and erected in A.D. 869. In

Stela 32, showing the face and headdress of a figure representing the Mexican rain god, Tlaloc.

Altar 12, the surface of which shows a seated figure within the jaws of a serpent, a very common theme in Tikal art.

between are a great number of monuments, many of which fall into fairly definite stylistic classes. For instance, Stelae 1, 2, and 28 all share the same wrap-around continuous design on front and sides with a text on the rear surface. All three are in the Tikal Museum. Unfortunately the texts give no clue to their carving dates but style suggests a date of about A.D. 400. Stela 4 on the North Terrace, Stela 18 in the Plaza, and Stela 29, just noted, all have in common a carved figure on the front, a text on the back, and plain sides. As a group they probably antedate Stelae 1, 2, and 28. Stelae 3, 6, 7, 8, 9, and 13 in the Great Plaza, and 15 in the West Plaza, as well as the distant Stela 27 (in an isolated spot about one-third of a mile north of the Tikal Museum) all have in common a single, relatively unadorned individual on the front, texts on both sides, and a plain back. This large group of monuments was set up around A.D. 480 to 500. This was followed by various sculptures, for instance, Stela 14, standing in the Great Plaza, and Stelae 23, 25, and 31, now in the Tikal Museum; with dates around A.D. 525, these monuments have the principal person on the front, flanking figures on the sides, and the main text on the back. Stelae 10 and 12 in the Great Plaza are almost twins, having essentially the same figure on the front, while the sides and back are covered with hieroglyphs. These monuments date from about A.D. 530. The fragmentary Stela 17, off the north edge of the East Plaza, has a date of about A.D. 555 and belongs to this same class of monument. Stela 17 is the latest known Early Classic monument at Tikal.

The bulk of the Late Classic stelae occur in the Twin-pyramid Complexes; these are Stelae 16, 19, 20, 22, and 30. Stela 24 stands in front of Temple III, Stela 5 in front of Structure 5D-33 of the North

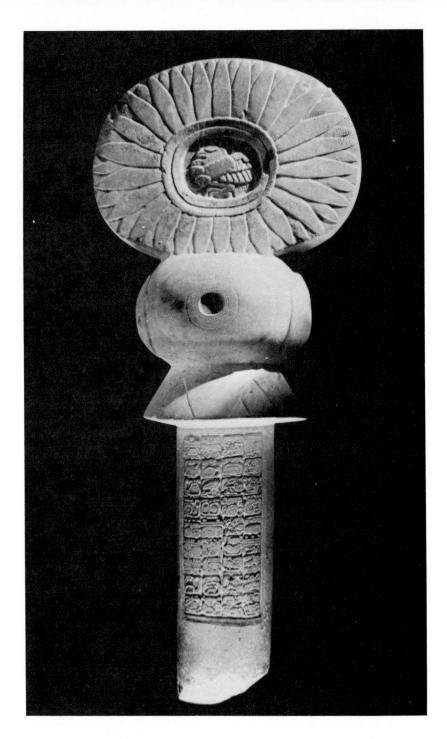

Ball Court marker found in Structure 6C-XVI. Now on exhibit in the National Museum of Guatemala.

Head of deity within the
gaping jaws of a jaguar,
a detail of Stela 28.

Stela 29,
the earliest monument
with a hieroglyphic text
known from Tikal.

Acropolis, Stela 21 in front of the Temple of the Inscriptions, and Stela 11, the latest, in the Great Plaza. On all Late Classic stelae the rear surface is uncarved. With the exceptions of Stelae 5 and 24, no hieroglyphs occur on the sides, and Stela 30 is unique in having no text at all. Stela 32, on exhibit in the Tikal Museum, is only a fragment, but an important one, for it portrays the Mexican rain deity, Tlaloc, in a guise essentially the same as that seen at Teotihuacán, northeast of Mexico City. It belongs to Early Classic times and comes from a huge trash pit intruded into the stairway of Structure 5D-26 up on the North Acropolis. The design on this stela is very close to that shown on a shield on the right side of the Early Classic Stela 31, also in the Tikal Museum.

Early Classic altars include numbers 3, 4, and 12, on the east end of the North Terrace and probably dating around A.D. 500. The incomplete Altar 13, found near Stela 29, is exhibited in the Tikal Museum and belongs to about this same time. Altar 19, Early Classic in date, is now shown in the Museum in front of Stela 31, with which it probably was originally paired. Late Classic altars occur with Stelae 5 and 11 in the Great Plaza and North Terrace, with Stela 24 in front of Temple III, with Stela 21 in front of the Temple of the Inscriptions, while five others occur with carved stelae in Twin-pyramid Complexes. Small fragments of other numbered altars, all Early Classic, are in Tikal Project storage.

THE GROWTH AND DECLINE OF TIKAL

On the preceding pages many of the architectural and sculptural remains of Tikal have been discussed. The majority of surface features belong to Late Classic times (A.D. 550-900). However, there are probably very few areas within central Tikal in which Preclassic (pre-A.D. 250) features do not lie buried under one's feet or interred beneath the relatively late structures that one sees. The beginnings of Tikal go back to at least 600 B.C.

Evidence from these earliest known times consists of rare deposits of trash and an occasional simple burial found over the years of excavation. These remains have been labeled as Eb, an arbitrarily selected term that applies to the pottery of those times (cuspidor-shaped vessels, neckless jars, and so forth). The Eb ceramic remains that have been accidentally found, for instance, on bedrock beneath the North Acropolis, include nothing that would preclude identification of these early Tikal people as Maya. Whether they were among the first to enter the vast forests of the Petén remains to be determined. One can only conjecture that the elevation of Tikal above the surrounding countryside, with its extensive seasonal swamps or *bajos*, would have been one of its attractions. Another probable stimulus to settlement here was the occurrence of extensive flint deposits. Undoubtedly Tikal became one of the outstanding if not the main workshop for flint implements in this part of the Maya area. We also know that these early Maya, besides having a quite sophisticated ceramic technology, had widespread trade connections, evidenced by imported obsidian and quartzite. Unfortunately nothing is known of their architecture because the Maya habitually destroyed, totally or in part, their earlier constructions to obtain fill for new building enterprises and also to expose bedrock for quarrying. Thus it is impossible to guess where such very early remains are to be found.

In time, ceramic styles evolved and new types of pottery vessels, designated Tzec, appeared about 500 B.C. and persisted some centuries until about 200 B.C. Excavations of this period have disclosed floors and burials as well as pottery, but buildings and distinct platforms of Tzec times have yet to be positively identified. They undoubtedly exist. It is simply a problem of penetrating enough later Preclassic and Classic construction to locate them. Their depth, coupled with the noted predilection of the Maya to destroy the old, is bound to make discovery of Tzec-related architecture difficult, if not a matter of pure luck. The distribution of Tzec pottery from testings indicates quite a wide distribution of peoples at the site during these centuries.

With the advent of Chuen pottery, about 200 B.C., archaeologists are certain that architecture of a ceremonial nature was being produced. The earliest versions of the North Acropolis date to Chuen

Heads from pottery figurines believed to be of Preclassic Chuen times. Center head, 3 ¹/₂ inches high.

Elaborately decorated vessel with spout, from a burial of Preclassic Cauac times. Height, 12 inches.

times, between 200 and 50 B.C. By perhaps 100 B.C. the North Acropolis had emerged as a platform measuring 75 by 90 feet, with four stairways across its seven-foot high south face, the whole supporting a variety of what appear to have been religious structures (but dismantled to make way for later construction). During these times the Great Plaza and North Terrace were as large and as formal as they were in Late Classic times, 600 to 700 years later. The remains of a simple house with a kitchen have been located for this period east of the Tikal Reservoir (15 minutes east of the Inn). There is every reason to infer that Tikal was a major site by this time, with a fairly large permanent population and most of the formal attributes of typical Maya ceremonialism.

Later, from 50 B.C. to about A.D. 150, during the period of Cauac pottery, Tikal grew more elaborate and ornate in its ritual architecture.

The North Acropolis, for example, underwent various revampings and rebuildings during Cauac times. Vaulted tombs, large temples with rich, polychromed stucco work and masks, as well as carved monuments (however fragmentary today) are some of the features of this Preclassic phase. A great portion of what followed in Classic times was simply an elaboration of what was then current. However, it has not been established that the Maya of Cauac Tikal yet had true hieroglyphic texts.

During the period of A.D. 150 to about 250 new forms of pottery, known as Cimi, appeared at Tikal, but these ceramic innovations did not change architectural patterns and other site characteristics as far as can be gauged. By A.D. 250 polychrome pottery incorporating three or more colors was being produced and traded. The use of corbelled vaults in architecture had also been achieved by then, if not earlier, thus marking the beginnings of what archaeologists refer to as the Classic Period. In retrospect, the whole Preclassic era, at Tikal 800 or more years in length, was one of beginnings, of formulation, and, surprisingly in many ways, maturation as well. One of the great problems of American archaeology has been that of determining the source of the major features of Maya culture, both in tangible products and in social, economic, and political organization. Many students feel that the ceremonial aspects of such early sites as Tikal owed their origin to influence, if not direct movements, of peoples from adjacent areas such as the Guatemala Valley, about Guatemala City, or even from the Olmec area of Gulf Coastal Mexico. Others insist that the features we see in early Tikal are not specifically dependent on contacts with other peoples and areas, but, instead, represent an early and brilliant Maya elaboration of basic traits generally common to much of Mesoamerica of that time. The art belonging to Tikal around 50 B.C. suggests strong interaction between highland and lowland Maya and that influence and stimulation operated in both directions.

During the Classic era at Tikal, from roughly A.D. 250 to 900, there was remarkably little artifactual change. Ceramics slowly evolved, shifting in form and decoration; monuments became larger and perhaps less ornate and correspondingly more formal; cached offerings and mortuary practices did shift as did architectural details and methods; but the old pattern of temple plan and the pattern long established in the ceremonial-administrative portions of Tikal were scarcely changed. Though impossible to prove as far as present knowledge of the site is concerned, it seems likely that population steadily increased as did the building of temple and palace clusters, with a network of causeways connecting the main parts of Tikal.

The Classic Maya of Tikal maintained an extensive trade, importing quantities of marine material from the coasts for ceremonial use, trading for masses of obsidian from the Highlands and for hematite, pyrite, amazonite, and jade from a variety of non-Lowland wources. Perhaps the most enigmatic aspect of Classic Tikal was its strong

Early Classic pottery vessel
in the form of a monkey.
Height, 7 $\frac{1}{2}$ inches.

Orange cylindrical tripod vessel,
a typical Early Classic form.
Height, 7 inches.

A lavishly
polychromed
basal-flange
bowl with
a modeled
jaguar head
as a handle.
A fine example
of Early Classic
ceramic art.
Diameter, 13 inches.

101

Only 4 ¹/₂ inches high,
an Early Classic figurine
masterfully fashioned of wood,
stucco, shell, and jade.

Lower right a stuccoed cylindrical
tripod vase, Teotihuacan style, with a
Classic maya head as the handle of
the cover.

Scene, 40 inches long, from an Early Classic vessel depicting the warriors and temples of Teotihuacán, found at Tikal among the reburied contents of a tomb.

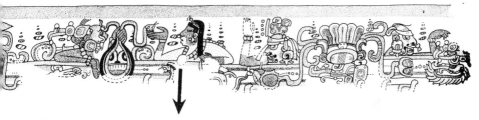

Photographic detail of the strange scene [shown above] minutely painted in black, red, yellow, and green on the plastered surface of an Early Classic wooden bowl. The design unrolls to 28 inches.

relationship with Teotihuacán, either directly or indirectly. The influence of this huge site, northeast of Mexico City, becomes apparent on monuments and in rich burials at Tikal of about A.D. 450-500. Three low four-stair platforms have been found with general characteristics of Teotihuacán-type architecture; these platforms appear to have been built no earlier than A.D. 600.

Another great problem centers on the correctness of the term "city," as so commonly applied to such sites as Tikal. Was Tikal essentially a city or did it function as a ceremonial center? A city —a term most difficult to define— can be thought of as a settlement incorporating permanent residence of a *relatively* large number of people, well organized with a multiplicity of functions (administrators, priests, traders, artisans, farmers, etc.), who lived *relatively* close to one another,

103

*Heads of Teotihuacán deities painted in rich colors
on a stuccoed vessel found in Tikal Burial 10. A.D. 450.*

*A throned ruler receiving dignitaries and an offering, painted on
a stuccoed Late Classic vessel. Length of design, about 20 inches.*

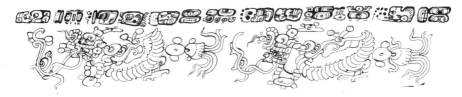

Two fantastic birds with necklaces and headdress seen on a Late Classic polychrome bowl.

Jade figure, 4 inches high,
from the tomb beneath Temple I.

Maya god incised on obsidian flake.
Such objects were made in
vast numbers for Late
Classic buried offerings.

with construction sufficiently compacted to provide some basis for circumscribing the community. In contrast, a ceremonial center usually seems to be thought of as a concentration of temples and palaces, as primarily a religious center, with a resident population essentially that of priests, attendants, high level administrators (if not the priests

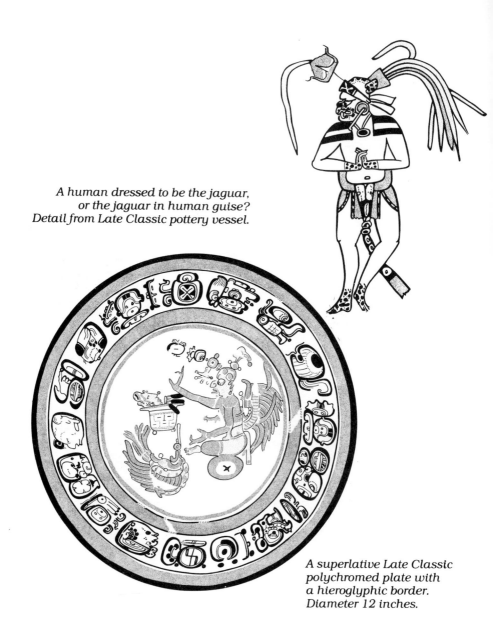

A human dressed to be the jaguar, or the jaguar in human guise? Detail from Late Classic pottery vessel.

A superlative Late Classic polychromed plate with a hieroglyphic border. Diameter 12 inches.

themselves), and specialists for the production of the paraphernalia necessary in the ceremonies; a ceremonial center may be thought of as a shrine, a pilgrimage and marketing center, to which people traveled on religious and commercial occasions —a center sustained by external contribution in the form of labor and produce, particularly from slash-and-burn, digging-stick maize agriculture. But, in the case of Tikal, there is no real reason to doubt that the bulk of the small structures within the roughly six square miles of mapped Tikal were in fact domestic units. Over 100 relatively small buildings that directly relate to residence have been investigated at Tikal. All but a very few of those excavated are Late Classic. The erratic topography of Tikal necessarily minimized dense concentrations of houses, if such was ever a Classic Maya inclination. The natural terrain of Tikal was an effective deterrent to achieving a street-gridded site. Houses instead were arranged largely in clusters on elevated terrain, usually about a small square plaza within each cluster or compound. Each compound, say, of four or five houses and outbuildings, could well have been occupied by an extended family. This would have included a family head or patriarch who would have occupied the most substantial residence with his immediate family, and whose sons and their families would have occupied the remaining houses of the group. Some houses were built substantially of stone and plaster, but usually they had thatched roofs rather than corbelled vaults. There is a great range of quality of house construction at Tikal. The ceramics and burials associated with houses also are most variable in quality. These differences suggest social and economic diversity among the residents of Tikal. There are many known cases of a family shrine being built on the east side of the family plaza. Here ceremonies were conducted and evidently important members of the family were interred. There were no graveyards as such at Tikal; at least none have been found. Most people were buried beneath the floors of the houses they had lived in. It has been estimted that *at least* 10,000 people were permanent residents of the mapped portion of Tikal. This estimate could be increased were it to be conclusively shown that the massive, abundant Tikal "palaces" (for instance, the Central Acropolis) were in fact residences of the more elite members of the community. While population density at Tikal was far less than, say, at Tenochtitlán (the Aztec capital at the time of the Conquest and now underlying Mexico City), there appear to be good grounds for assessing Tikal as something more than a ceremonial center. Its characteristics were not so markedly urban as those of Tenochtitlán, but Tikal did have many elements of an urban level or way of living. But whether it was a "city" or not, will undoubtedly be argued for a long time to come.

Central Tikal has been mapped. Much remains to be done in studying and understanding what lies peripheral to these almost six square miles. A frequent question is, What are the actual limits of Tikal? Preliminary survey indicated a noticeable fall-off of house structures between Tikal and Uaxactun, five hours on foot north of Tikal. About one mile west of Temple IV is a large group, Chikin Tikal, which consists of "palaces" and temples, even a causeway connecting the two major groups of this important site. The intervening area is sparse in house structures as most of it is *bajo* country. Uolantun, though smaller, is another nearby important site. Other close "satellites" of Tikal include Jimbal, El Encanto, Bobal, Corozal, and El Palmar. But at what point Tikal ends and something else begins is most difficult to

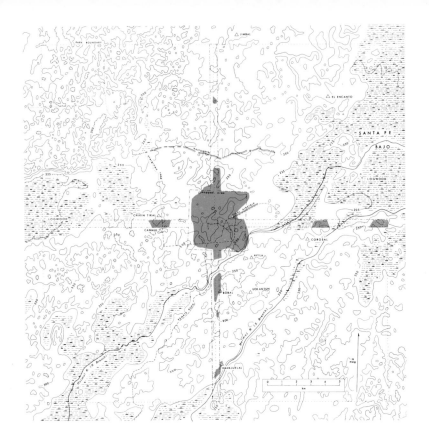

Overall map of the Tikal National Park which covers an area of 576 square kilometers. Surveyed strips carry to the Park boundaries. Colored areas mark terrain in which remains of ancient occupation are relatively abundant. The earth embankment is shown here running east and west just north of central Tikal (colored square at center, a detailed view of which is shown on the guide map accompanying this handbook).

specify. Although Tikal and Uaxactun had a great deal in common, there were important, often subtle differences between these two not overly distant centers, suggesting that, despite the apparent dominance of Tikal, Uaxactun inherently had or was permitted a certain amount of latitude in artistic and ceremonial matters. In other words, there probably are cultural boundaries to be considered. Then there is the question of sustaining population, that is, the people living about such great centers whose corn fields directly contributed to the economic sustenance of sites like Tikal. The orientation of the farming population to one site or another thus forms still another problem in trying to understand the structure of Maya living about Tikal. In short, when in Tikal one knows that anyone living there was part of its population, but, traveling out farther and farther from the center, it becomes increasingly difficult to decide whether people populating the periphery were truly connected with central Tikal.

In order to know more securely what lies about known Tikal, archaeologists undertook systematic explorations along specially cut trails radiating out 7 $1/2$ miles from the Great Plaza. House structures and intermittent small ceremonial and administrative nuclei are found to abound miles out from Tikal. Mapping indicates that these decrease in frequency to the north and south of central Tikal. In 1966, two and a half miles north of the Great Plaza, a combined wall and ditch was discovered running almost six miles east-west before disappearing in swampy areas. Built and renovated during Classic times, it is oriented towards Uaxactun to the north, and has been cogently argued as being a defense. All in all, there are good signs that ancient Tikal had limits and that the area it encompassed was larger than ever suspected. Including large tracts of uninhabited *bajos,* or swamps, it is possible, judging from preliminary clues, that Tikal may have grown to a size of some 25 square miles.

As this work continues, so does analysis of the excavation data gained from large areas of central Tikal in which prior mapping failed to record construction, for instance, in the form of small mounds. It is now clear that these areas can be only superficially vacant. Digging in them has revealed considerable evidence of human occupation in the way of quarries, disturbed living refuse, chultuns, as well as small habitation mounds of such simple makeup as to leave little to no surface sign of them today.

Without the staggeringly difficult work of exploring and mapping all that lies about Tikal and without the unglamorous probing for what may lie in the otherwise blank areas spotted throughout central Tikal, there would be few grounds for estimating what the whole of ancient Tikal was like. Work such as this balances the other emphasis on temples, tombs, palaces, and monuments.

Reasonable questions as to how and why Tikal grew to what it became and what it really was in terms of social existence are not served by easy answers. Equally difficult to answer is why Tikal and all its Classic ramifications came to an end. This is really a matter of the collapse of lowland Maya civilization. Note has been made on the preceding pages of unfinished construction, such as the small abandoned temple in the West Plaza. Everything that is known points to a rapid disintegration of Classic authority and direction. What the actual causes were and why they had their effect when they did, about A.D. 900, are frankly unanswered by excavation. If archaeologists had a better grasp of what went on in Classic times —how people were organized among themselves and in relation to their environment— the seeds or preconditions of collapse might be better identified. A variety of theoretical causes has been proposed over the last half century of Maya studies, ranging from the naturally catastrophic (earthquake, pestilence, etc.) to one concerning relationships between population and agricultural productivity, and even cultural exhaustion or decadence as an inherent trend of civilization. Earthquake is a simple explanation, but there is no evidence to support it even as a minor factor in the collapse. It must be realized that collapse was not localized to Tikal or the immediate region of which it was a part. The breakup of Classic authority and the disappearance of a Classic way of life held true throughout the lowland Maya cities, centers, and hamlets, from Palenque in Mexico to Copán in Honduras and north far beyond Tikal. In searching for an answer, there are a great many variables to be considered: for instance, an expanding population and a correspondingly decreasing agricultural productivity (primarily of corn) through reasons of land exhaustion; political strife or internal power struggles without an adequate economic base; outright decimation or eviction of the ruling groups by a peasantry increasingly aware of the progressively more ponderous burden of Maya ceremonialism and the demands of the ruling class —a peasantry perhaps influenced by the social turbulence and militaristic trends then current in Mexico; and so on and so forth from one theory to another. One can almost assume, given the implicit complexity of Maya culture during Classic, even late Preclassic times, that the causes were far from simple. We can only speculate as to the reasons for abandoned construction at Tikal and the end of fashioning monuments. Essentially everything thought of by us as Classic ceases and what remains for a few hundred years thereafter is a decadent, limpid reflection of what once had been. The activities of Postclassic survivors and successors at Tikal have been noted on prior pages: the ransacking of tombs and cached offerings, the movement of monuments and the attempts to maintain a semblance of the ancient monument cult in the Great Plaza and elsewhere. By any standards this was truly the end of a great civilization.

*Modeled-carved pottery vessel,
typical of the times,
from a Postclassic grave.
Height, 8 ¹/₂ inches.
Scene shows two consulting rulers.*

APPENDIX

Maya Methods of Dating at Tikal

The basic calendar of the ancient Mesoamericans, which the Maya of Tikal shared, consisted of a time cycle of 52 years, or 18,980 days. Scholars term this cycle the Calendar Round. The Maya term for this round remains unknown. The Maya and other Mesoamericans counted vigesimally in ordinary matters, that is, by increments of twenty, rather than decimally. The simplest Maya method of recording numbers was a dot for "1" and a bar for "5." Head variants for numbers were also used. After 19 (3 bars and 4 dots), zero was reached, followed by 1, then 2, and so forth, to 19 again. Numbers were noted positionally, as we positionally record 1's, 10's, 100's, and so forth from right to left. Zero was conceived of as completion in one sense and as beginning in another and was indicated in the codices, or books, as a conventionalized shell and, on the monuments, by an elaborated quatrefoil, often partially obscured.

The *Calendar Round* results from the permutation or meshing of three basic cycles, the *Sacred Round*, itself made up of two cycles, and the *Vague Year*. The Sacred Round consists of one cycle of 13 numbered days (1-13) and a second cycle of 20 named days. The permutation of the two results in a total of 260 combinations of day numbers and names (13 × 20 = 260). The Vague Year on the other hand comprises 365 days that come about by allowing 18 so-called months of 20 days each (numbered 0-19) and an extra 5 days (18 × 20 + 1 × 5 = 365). While the Sacred Round was employed only to reckon ceremonial matters, the Vague Year closely approximates by intention the solar year.

If, for instance, today is a 4 Ahau Cumku ("4 Ahau" being a day within the Sacred Round and "8 Cumkú the eighth day within the "month" Cumku within the Vague Year), it will require the passage of 52 years, or 18,980 days, for the day named 4 Ahau 8 Cumku to reappear. This is so according to a simple mathematical principle of permutation (260 and 365 have 5 as their common divisor; thus, 5 × 52 × 73 = 18,980). Many Mesoamerican peoples operated with this calendar which was precise to the day over a period of 52 years. What the Maya did was to devise a calendar that incorporated the Calendar Round principle and that allowed positioning of events to the day far beyond the limits imposed by the relative brevity of a Calendar Round. The method they devised was the Long Count, or *Initial Series*.

Positional notation, vigesimal counting (by 20's), and reckoning from a base date (as we do in terms of the birth of Christ) are the characteristics of the Initial Series. The common Maya time units, positionally arranged were as follows:

Baktun	=	144,000 days (or 20 Katuns)
Katun	=	7,200 days (or 20 Tuns)
Tun	=	360 days (or 18 Uinals)
Uinal	=	20 days (or 20 Kins)
Kin	=	1 day

The only discrepancy in the matter of vigesimal counting occurs here in the Tun which was made 5 days short of the Vague Year of 365 days by giving it the value of 18 Uinals. In an Initial Series statement, the Baktun, according to the positional rule, precedes the Katun, and the Katun the Tun, and so forth.

The first notation in such a statement is the *Initial Series Introducing Glyph*. With a few exceptions, this glyph alerts us to the fact that this total number of days, expressed in the following recorded numbers of Baktuns, Katuns, etc., has elapsed since the beginning of the Maya calendar. In the Initial Series the point most commonly employed by the Maya as the beginning date, or base or zero date, was 4 Ahau 8 Cumku, a single day within a Calendar Round. Why this day among the 18,980 possibilities was chosen as a standard is unknown. The Long Count or Initial Series method of dating amounts to nothing more than a statement of the elapsed interval of time (in specific numbers of Baktuns, Katuns, etc.) *from* a standard beginning date, way in the past, *to* the terminal date which is thus located in time. This beginning date can only be reckoned in Christian time by choosing one of the several competing Maya-Christian calendrical correlation theories. The generally favored correlation, according to some experts (see below), places this Calendar Round day, 4 Ahau 8 Cumku, in 3113 B.C. This is not to say that the Maya invented the Long Count method on this date. Even the rough date of invention is controversial. However it was certainly millennia later in time than the date agreed upon by its inventors as the starting point in their Long Count calculations.

Most of the recorded dates on monuments at Tikal and other Maya sites are associated with Baktun 9, that is 9 x 144,000 days after the base date, 4 Ahau 8 Cumku. Others are known from Baktuns 8 and 10. During the centuries that Baktun 9 was being recorded on monuments and the like, Baktun 9 had actually ended, and Baktun 10 was running its course. But archaeologists by convention consider events to have occurred "during" or "within" Baktun 9 when this period of time is recorded on monuments. (We follow an identical course: the year 1967 indicates that 19 centuries have been completed and we are now in the sixty-seventh year of the 20th century). Practically everything seen at Tikal by the visitor was in this sense created during Baktun 9. Baktun 9 began (in the most reasonable correlation; see below) on the (Gregorian) day December 9, A.D. 435 and ended

*Stela 3 text
with the Initial
Series shaded*

March 13, 830. It happens to have encompassed the great portion of Classic time.

Turning to one example, Stela 3 of Tikal, we can see that the Long Count date 9.2.13.0.0 is recorded in the form of 9 Baktuns, 2 Katuns, 13 Tuns, 0 (or completed) Uinals, and 0 (or completed) Kins. This text appears on the observed right side of the stela. The Initial Series Introducing Glyph and the period glyphs (Baktun, Katun, etc.) are arranged typically to be read from left side to right side, and top row to second row, and so forth on down. The glyphs used for these periods (Baktuns, Katuns, etc.) are recognizable to the specialist, even were there doubt as to the order of reading. The numbers, or coefficients, appear over each period glyph, with a 9 (1 bar and 4 dots) over the Baktun glyph, a 2 over the Katun, a 13 over the Tun, and a 0 over each of the Uinal and Kin glyphs. Scholars conventionally transcribe this Initial Series text as 9.2.13.0.0. This amount of time has elapsed from the base date 4 Ahau 8 Cumku. The calculation is as follows:

9 Baktuns (Baktun = 144,000 days)	=	1,296,000 days
2 Katuns (Katun = 7,200 days)	=	14,400 days
13 Tuns (Tun = 360 days)	=	4,680 days
0 Uinals (Uinal = 20 days)	=	0 days
0 Kins (Kin = 1 day)	=	0 days
Total elapsed number of days from base date 4 Ahau 8 Cumku	=	1,315,080 days

Conveniently this inscription goes on to tell us, as do most such inscriptions, to what day within the current Calendar Round (52-year cycle) 1,315,080 days exactly lead. This day in the Calendar Round is expressed on this stela in the following manner: The Sacred Round day, 4 Ahau, is carved immediately following the 0 Kin glyph block, while the Vague Year day, 13 Kayab, is the sixth glyph block beyond the Sacred Round day in the inscription. The intervening glyph blocks, five in number here, form what is called the Supplementary Series (see below). The Long Count inscription on Stela 3 tells us that so many days have passed between 4 Ahau 8 Cumku, far in the past, and a Calendar Round day, 4 Ahau 13 Kayab, recorded for some reason on this stela. Other Mesoamerican people had the capacity for placing an event within a 52-year period (as does the ending date, 4 Ahau 13 Kayab, on Stela 3), but the Maya had the means to say where in time, far beyond the brief limits of 52 years, that day belonged. The Maya discovered how to position these relatively short Calendar Round cycles within what some experts believe to have been a huge cycle of time, of 13 Baktuns duration, or 5200 Tuns, or 1,872,000 days.

The previously mentioned *Supplementary Series,* occurring between the Sacred Round and Vague Year glyph blocks, consists of a variable number of glyph blocks. A Supplementary Series may be wholly made up of a *Lunar Series* of from two to seven glyph blocks which may tell us the age within the current lunation, the length of the current moon (29 or 30 days, as recorded) and its position in groups of lunations.

A *Secondary Series* may follow the Initial Series and the Supplementary Series and it comprises one or more period glyphs. These glyphs give the time distance between pairs of dates. A Secondary Series may serve to link a later or earlier date with the one preceding it in the text, for example, the Initial Series date itself.

It has been proposed among various possibilities that the Secondary Series corrects for the measurable slip between the Vague Year and the solar year. Theoretical purposes of the Secondary Series also include recording historical events (births and accessions to power of rulers), astronomical phenomena, esoterica, dedicatory dates, and, as noted, the discrepancy between solar and Maya years. That texts and monuments on which they occur may directly relate to the rulers and their reigns is one of the most exciting aspects of hieroglyphic research today. The subject of *Dedicatory Date* arises when we ask, for example, when a particular monument was carved and installed. A Dedicatory Date may be established directly by the Initial Series (as well as by Period End and Short Count dates; see below) or by the date ultimately reached by one or more Secondary Series.

On occasion the Maya employed periods in their calculations above and beyond the Baktun. While the Baktun consists of 400 Tuns, or 20 Katuns, the *Pictun* had a value of 8,000 Tuns, the *Calabtun* 160,000

Tuns, and the *Kinchiltun* was equivalent to 3,200,000 Tuns, that is, 1,152,000,000 days. The observed right side of Stela 10 at Tikal has a single column of glyph blocks. In this column occurs a possible Initial Series statement of 1 Kinchiltun (the seventh glyph block from the top of the column), 11 Calabtuns, 19 Pictuns, 9 Baktuns, 3 Katuns, 11 Tuns, and 2 Uinals (the Kin glyph probably occurred on the now heavily eroded rear of the stela). Disregarding the Kin value (which, by rule, could not have exceeded 19 days), this text refers to the impressive total of 1,841,641,600 days¡ There is considerable uncertainty as to the function of this text. However, at other sites there are texts that exceed even this one in the amount of time recorded.

The Maya neverthless were not averse to short-cuts in recording dates. A dating method termed *Period End* was quite prevalent during Classic times. At Tikal in some cases (for example, Stela 4) a numbered Tun (360 days) is simply said to have ended on a particular Calendar Round day. The scholar has to calculate the Katun associated with the just-ended Tun, while the Baktun may be supplied from such considerations as the style and context of the stela. Other texts (for example, on Tikal stelae 16, 19, 20, and 22) record the Period Ends of particular Katuns. In these cases the Maya knew they were "within" a certain Baktun, thus it could be suppressed. If they wished as they frequently did, to conmemorate on a monument the completion of a certain Katun, say, of Baktun 9, there was no reason to enter the Tuns, Uinals and Kins, as each necessarily had the value of zero (a Katun could not end without the lesser periods completed as well). A Period End date (for instance, on Stela 22; see p. 86) could be reduced to a three-glyph block statement of the numbered Katun that was ended and on what day in the Calendar Round it terminated. Three glyphs (day, month, Katun), in the case of a Katun-end, told the Maya everything, as long as they mentally supplied the Baktun in which this Katun ended. This was a greatly abbreviated method of dating, but within an Initial Series context.

Another method of dating, but outside the Initial Series (or Long Count), was the *Short Count.* This method depends on the fact that each and every Katun ends on a day Ahau, numbered 1 through 13, in the Sacred Round. For instance, during Late Classic times, the Initial Series 9.17.0.0.0 ("17" referring to Katun 17) ends on the Sacred Round day 13 Ahau; 9.18.0.0.0 ends on 11 Ahau; 9.19.0.0.0 ends on 9 Ahau; and so forth, the Ahau day-number decreasing by two each successive Katun. While the Initial Series date 9.17.0.0.0 would be reduced in the Period End method to "Katun 17, 13 Ahau 18 Cumku," the completion of this same Katun in the Short Count method would be simply stated as "Katun 13 Ahau." However, a Katun can end on a 13 Ahau every 13 Katuns or 260 Tuns, equivalent to about 256 = solar years, and, thus, a katun 2 Ahau, or a Katun 13 Ahau, etc., necessarily recurs every 13 Katuns of time. Incidentally, the fact that 20 Katuns, or 260 Tuns, are close to 256 $\frac{1}{4}$ years long is due to a Tun being 360 days

Altar 14

long (that is, 18 uinals of 20 days each) rather than 365 $\frac{1}{4}$ days, the term of the solar year.

The only fairly clear example of a Short Count at Tikal is Altar 14 which records a large central 8 Ahau. Here, however, the Maya carved around the Ahau the actual Long Count date, 9.13.0.0.0. Neverthless, it is the Short Count that has been partly responsible for a major problem, namely the correlation of the Maya and Christian calendars.

Had the Maya in Postclassic times (after A.D. 900) continued until the Spanish Conquest of Yucatán to record matters in the Initial Series method, there would be no problem of correlation today. Those, like Bishop Landa (the 16th Century Spanish priest who recorded so much of Yucatán), could have asked a Maya scribe or scholar what the Long Count and Calendar Round date was for some day whose position was known in Christian time. However the Maya at the Conquest were employing only the Short Count and Calendar Round. Among students, who allow historical controls on the correlation, there is agreement that a Katun 13 Ahau ended near A.D. 1542, the founding date of Mérida, Yucatán. One problem has been to settle on the exact Christian day when Katun 13 Ahau ended and its successor, Katun 11 Ahau, began. The other problem has been to pin down this Katun 13 Ahau by the Long Count method. The principal Long Count dates most favored to achieve this correlation are the dates 11.16.0.0.0 and 12.9.0.0.0, the respective Katuns of which do in fact end on a 13 Ahau. These yield what are familiarly known as the "11.16" and the "12.9" correlations. Arguments have long centered on which is correct and on which variety of which proposed correlation best positions Katun 13 Ahau in Christian day, month, and year.

As stated, the main correlation contenders are the "11.16" and "12.9" "families." Each family covers modified versions separated by as little as a single day. It must be kept in mind that the 11.16 family provides about 260 real years less time than the 12.9 contenders for what happened prior to the Conquest. An extraordinary amount of data has been brought forward to preclude one correlation in favor of the other; for instance, survivals of the ancient calendar among certain highland Maya peoples. But the formidable literature on the subject of Maya-Christian correlation basically comes down to fixing in Christian time about 1,200 years of variously recorded Maya time and the events that took place in that chronological system.

At Tikal, as long as one works in contexts associated with Maya calendric texts, there is no problem, for Maya time handles dating very well. The difficulties emerge when working at Tikal in Preclassic and Postclassic contexts, so far lacking in useful evidence of Maya calendrics. Moreover, the moment charcoal or wood from a Classic source is submitted for radiocarbon dating, the whole problem of correlation becomes inescapable. This is true, since the results of the radiocarbon laboratory are given in the Christian system, which then have to be fitted to the Maya system of recording time.

On the whole, most evidence supports the "11.16" correlation as the correct one. It has passed the bulk of the historical, astronomical, archaeological, and radiocarbon tests to which it has been submitted. This does not mean that all experts are agreed on its being the correct one. For instance, an archaeologist may find tht so much went on in his Postclassic (really for the most part post-Initial Series) sequence that more time is required to fit it all in. The "12.9" correlation gives him about 260 extra years to permit what he believes to have happened. And so it goes. It is an absorbing problem that one doubts can ever be solved to the satisfaction of all.

Graffito, of a Procession from Maler's Palace

SELECTED BIBLIOGRAPHY

Publications of Tikal Project

Adams, R. E. W., and A. S. Trik
    1961   Temple I (Str. 5D-1): Post-constructional activities. Tikal Report No. 7, *Museum Monographs, The University Museum.* Philadelphia.

Carr, R. F., and J. E. Hazard
    1961   Map of the ruins of Tikal, El Petén, Guatemala. Tikal Report No. 11. *Museum Monographs, The University Museum.* Philadelphia.

Coe, W. R.
    1958   Two carved lintels from Tikal, *Archaeology,* Vol. 11, No. 2, pp. 75-80. Cambridge.
    1959   Tikal 1959. *Expedition,* Vol. 1, No. 4, pp. 7-12. Philadelphia.
    1962a   Maya mystery in Tikal. *Natural History.* New York. Part I, Vol. 71, No. 7, pp. 10-12, August-September. Part II. Vol. 71, No. 8, pp. 44-53, October.
    1962b   Priestly power and peasant corn: Excavations and reconstructions at Tikal. *Illustrated London News.* London. Part I, Vol. 240, No. 6390, pp. 103-106, January 20. Part II, Vol. 240, No. 6391, pp. 135-137, January 27.
    1962c   A summary of excavation and research at Tikal, Guatemala: 1956-1961. *American Antiquity,* Vol. 27, No. 4, pp. 479-507. Salt Lake City.
    1963a   Current Research (Tikal). *American Antiquity,* Vol. 28, No. 3, pp. 417-419. Salt Lake City.
    1963b   A summary of excavation and research at Tikal, Guatemala: 1962. *Estudios de Cultura Maya,* Vol. III, pp. 41-64. Mexico.
    1964   Current Research (Tikal). *American Antiquity,* Vol. 29, No. 3, pp. 411-413. Salt Lake City.
    1965a   Tikal, Guatemala, and emergent Maya civilization. *Science,* Vol. 147, No. 3664, pp. 1401-1419. Washington.
    1965b   Current Research (Tikal). *American Antiquity,* Vol. 30, No. 3, pp. 379-383. Salt Lake City.
    1965c   Tikal: Ten Years of Study of a Maya Ruin in the Lowlands of Guatemala. *Expedition,* Vol. 8, No. 1. Philadelphia.

Coe, W. R., and V. L. Broman
    1958   Excavations in the Stela 23 group. Tikal Report No. 2, *Museum Monographs, The University Museum.* Philadelphia.

Coe, W. R., and J. J. McGinn
    1963   The North Acropolis of Tikal and an early tomb. *Expedition,* Vol. 5, No. 2, pp. 24-32. Philadelphia.

Coe, W. R., E. M. Shook, and L. Satterthwaite
    1961   The carved wooden lintels of Tikal. Tikal Report No. 6. *Museum Monographs, The University Museum.* Philadelphia.

Coe, W. R., and W. S. Haviland
    1982   Introduction to the Archaeology of Tikal, Guatemala. TIKAL REPORT No. 12. University museum monograph 46; the University Museum, University of Pennsylvania, U.S.A.

Coe, W. R., E. M. Shook, and L. Satterthwaite
    1961   The carved wooden lintels of Tikal. Tikal Report No. 6. *Museum Monographs, The University Museum.* Philadelphia.

Culbert, T. P.
    1963   Ceramic research at Tikal, Guatemala. *Cerámica de Cultura Maya,* Vol. 1, Nos. 2 and 3, pp. 34-42, Cambridge, Mass.

Dyson, R. H., Jr.
    1962   The Tikal Project-1962. *Archaeology,* Vol. 15, No. 2, pp. 131-132. New York.

Greene, Virginia, and H. Moholy-Nagy
    1966   A Teotihuacan-style vessel from Tikal: A correction. *American Antiquity.* Vol. 31, No. 3, Part I, p. 432.

Harrison, P. D.
    1963   A jade pendant from Tikal. *Expedition,* Vol. 5, No. 2, pp. 12-13. Philadelphia.

Haviland, W. A.
    1962   A "Miniature stela" from Tikal. *Expedition,* Vol. 4, No. 3, pp. 2-3. Philadelphia.
    1965   Prehistoric settlement at Tikal, Guatemala. *Expedition,* Vol. 7, No. 3, pp. 14-23. Philadelphia.

Jones C. and L. Satterthwaite
    1982   The Monumentes and Inscriptions of Tikal: The Carver Monuments. TIKAL REPORT No. 33 Part. "A". Series Editors: W.R. Coe and W. A. Haviland. University museum monograph 44. The University Museum, University of Pennsylvania.

Moholy-Nagy, H.
    1962   A Tlaloc stela from Tikal. *Expedition,* Vol. 4, No. 2 p. 27. Philadelphia.

1963a   The field laboratory at Tikal. *Expedition*, Vol. 5, No. 3, pp. 12-17. Philadelphia.

1963b   Shells and other marine material from Tikal. *Estudios de Cultura Maya*, Vol. III, pp. 65-83. Mexico.

1965   Tikal mosaic statuettes. *Archaeology*, Vol. 19, No. 2, pp. 84-89. New York.

Puleston, Dennis E.

1965   The chultuns of Tikal. *Expedition*, Vol. 7, No. 3, pp. 24-29. Philadelphia.

1983   The Settlement Survey of Tikal. TIKAL REPORT No. 13. Volume Editor: W. A. Haviland, Series Editors: W. R. Coe and W. A. Haviland. University Museum Monograph 48 the University Museum, University of Pennsylvania, U.S.A.

Puleston, Dennis E., and D. W. Callender, Jr.

1967   Defensive earthworks at Tikal. *Expedition*, Vol. 9, No. 3, pp. 40-48. Philadelphia.

Rainey, F. G.

1956   The Tikal Project. *University Museum Bulletin*, Vol. 20, No. 4, pp. 2-24. Philadelphia.

Satterthwaite, L.

1956   Maya dates on stelae in Tikal "enclosures," *University Museum Bulletin*, Vol. 20, No. 4, pp. 25-40. Philadelphia.

1958a   The problem of abnormal stela placements at Tikal and elsewhere. Tikal Report No. 3, *Museum Monographs, The University Museum*. Philadelphia.

1958b   Five newly discovered carved monuments at Tikal and new data on four others. Tikal Report No. 4, *Ibid.*

1960   Maya "Long Count" numbers. *Expedition*, Vol. 2, No. 2, pp. 36-37. Philadelphia.

1963   Note on hieroglyphs on bone from the tomb below Temple I, Tikal. *Expedition, Vol. 6, No. 1, pp. 18-19. Philadelphia.*

1964   *Dates in a new Tikal hieroglyphic text as katun-baktun anniversaries. Estudios de Cultura Maya*, Vol. IV. Mexico.

Satterthwaite, L., V. L. Broman, and W. A. Haviland

1961   Miscellaneous investigations: Excavation near Fragment 1 of Stela 17, with observations on Stela P34 and Miscellaneous Stone 25; excavation of Stela 25, Fragment 1; excavation of Stela 27; excavation of Stela 28, Fragment 1. Tikal Report No. 8. *Museum Monographs, The University Museum*. Philadelphia.

Satterthwaite, L., and E. K. Ralph

1960   New radiocarbon dates and the Maya correlation problem. *American Antiquity*, Vol. 26, No. 2, pp. 165-184. Salt Lake City.

Shook, E. M.

1957   The Tikal Project. *The University Museum Bulletin*,
        Vol. 21, No. 3, pp. 36-52. Philadelphia.

1958a   Field Director's report: The 1956 and 1957 seasons.
        Tikal Report No. 1. *Museum Monographs, The Univer-
        sity Museum.* Philadelphia.

1958b   The Temple of the Red Stela. *Expedition*, Vol. 1, No. 1,
        pp. 26-33. Philadelphia. (Spanish transltion in *Antro-
        pologia e Historia de Guatemala*, Vol. 11, No. 2,
        pp. 7-14. Guatemala, 1958.)

1960   Tikal Stela 29. *Expedition*, Vol. 2, No. 2, pp. 28-35.
        Philadelphia.

1962   Tikal: Problems of a Field Director. *Expedition*, Vol. 4,
        No. 2, pp. 11-26. Philadelphia.

1964   Archaeological investigations in Tikal, Petén, Gua-
        temala. *Actas y Memorias del XXXV Congreso Inter-
        nacional de Americanistas, Mexico, 1962*, Vol. I,
        pp. 279-386. Mexico.

Shook, E. M., and W. R. Coe

1961   Tikal: Numeration, terminology, and objectives. Tikal
        Report No. 5. *Museum Monographs, The University
        Museum.* Philadelphia.

Shook, E. M., and A. Kidder II

1961   The Painted Tomb at Tikal. *Expedition*, Vol. 4, No. 1,
        pp. 2-7. Philadelphia.
        (Spanish translation in *Antropologia e Historia de
        Guatemala*, Vol. 14, No. 1, pp. 5-10. Guatemala, 1962.)

Stuckenrath, Robert, Jr., W. R. Coe, and E. K. Ralph

1966   University of Pennsylvania Radiocarbon Dates IX: Tikal
        Series. Guatemala. *Radiocarbon*, Vol. 8, pp. 371-385.

Trik, A. S.

1963   The splendid tomb of Temple I at Tikal Guatemala.
        Expedition, Vol. 6, No. 1, pp. 2-18. Philadelphia.

Trik, Helen and M. E. Kampen

1983   The Graffiti of Tikal. TIKAL REPORT No. 31, Volume
        editor: W. R. Coe and W. A. Haviland. University
        Museum Monograph 57. The University Museum,
        University of Pennsylvania.

Webster, H. T.

1963   Tikal graffiti. *Expedition*, Vol. 6, No. 1, pp. 36-47.
        Philadelphia.

Other Publications

Barthel, T. S.
    1963   Die Stele 31 von Tikal. *Tribus*, No. 12, pp. 159-214.
            Stuttgart.
Basch, P. F.
    1959   Land mollusca of the Tikal National Park, Guatemala.
            Occasional Papers of the Museum of Zoology, University of Michigan, No. 612. Ann Arbor.
Berlin, Heinrich
    1951   El templo de las inscripciones-VI-de Tikal. *Antropología e Historia de Guatemala*, Vol. 3, No. 1, pp. 33-54.
            Guatemala.
    1963   A new temple at Tikal. *Archaeology*, Vol. 6, No. 2, pp. 82-86. Brattleboro.
Beyer, H.
    1943   Algunos datos sobre los dinteles mayas de Tikal en el Museo Etnográfico de Basilia. *Proceedings of the 27th International Congress of Americanists*, Mexico, Vol. 1, pp. 338-343. Mexico.
Borhegyi, S. F., and S. Borhegyi
    1960   Pyramids in the jungle. *Lore*, Vol. 11, No. 1, pp. 22-28.
            Milwaukee.
Castañeda Paganini, R.
    1958   *Tikal: La ciudad arqueológica más grande de la civilización maya*. Ministerio de Educación Pública.
            Guatemala.
Cerezo Dardón, H.
    1951   Breve historia de Tikal. *Antropología e Historia de Guatemala*. Vol. 3, No. 1, pp. 1-8. Guatemala.
Cowgill, U. M.
    1963   El Bajo de Santa Fe. *Transaction of the American Philosophical Society*, Vol. 53, Part 7. Philadelphia.
Fernández, M. A.
    1939   Los dinteles de zapote y el secreto de como fueron tallados. *Proceedings of the 27th Interntional Congress of Americanists, Mexico*, Vol. 1, Part 1, pp. 601-611. Mexico.
Fialko, Vilma
    1987   El marcador de Juego de Pelota de Tikal: Nuevas Referencias Epigráficas para el Clásico Temprano. *Primer Simposio mundial sobre Epigrafía Maya*, pp. 61-80, Asociación Tikal. Guatemala.
Gosner, K. L.
    1952   Maya metropolis. *Natural History*, Vol. 61, pp. 104-109. New York.

Haberland, W.
1961   Tikal-Grossprojekt der Maya Archaologie. Umschau, Vol. 5, pp. 129-132. Frankfurt/Main.
Jerabek, C.
1959   Tikal-*Guatemala Tourist Guide.* Guatemala.
1963   *Maya ruins, Tikal:* A story-guidebook. Guatemala. Revised second edition.
Laporte, J.P. and V. Fialko
1985   Reporte Arqueológico: Mundo Perdido y Zona Habitacional. Proyecto Nacional Tikal, Instituto Nacional de Antropología e Historia de Guatemala.
Larios C. R. y M. Orrego
1983   Reporte de Las Investigaciones Arqueológicas en el Grupo 5E-11, Tikal.
        Instituto de Antropología e Historia de Guatemala.
Long, R.C.E.
1940   The dates on Altar 5 at Tikal. *American Antiquity,* Vol. 5, No. 4, pp. 283-286. Menasha.
Lundell, C.L.
1961   The flora of Tikal. *Expedition,* Vol. 3, No. 2, pp. 38-43. Philadelphia.
Maler, T.
1911   Explorations in the department of Petén, Guatemala: Tikal. *Memoirs, Peabody Museum, Harvard University,* Vol. 5, No. 1. Cambridge, Mass.
Méndez, M.
1955   Descubrimiento de las ruinas de Tikal. Informe del Corregidor del Petén Modesto Méndez, de 6 de marzo de 1848. *Antropología e Historia de Guatemala,* Vol. 7, No. 1, pp. 3-7. Guatemala.
Parson, M. J.
1964   Maya temple adventure. *Lore,* Vol. 14, No. 2, pp. 64-69. Milwaukee.
Ritzenthaler, R.E.
1957   Flight to Tikal, *Lore,* Vol. 7, No. 4, pp. 128-133. Milwaukee.
Schaeffer, E.
1951   El corregidor del Petén Coronel Modesto Méndez y el encargado de negocios de Prusia von Hesse. *Antropología e Historia,* Vol. 3, No. 1, pp. 55-60. Guatemala.
Seler, E.
1939   The cedrela slabs of Tikal in the museum at Basel. Reprinted in *Collected Works,* Vol. 1, Part 3, No. 23, Cambridge, Mass.
Shook, E.M.
1951   Investigaciones arqueológicas en las ruinas de Tikal, Departamento de El Petén, Guatemala. *Antropología e*

historia, Vol. 3, No. 1, pp. 9-32. Guatemala.

Smithe, F. B.
    1959   *Birds of Tikal: A Check List.* New York (privately printed).
    1966   *The Birds of Tikal.* Garden City.

Smithe, F.B., and R. A. Paynter, Jr.
    1963   Birds of Tikal, Guatemala. *Bulletin of the Museum of Comparative Zoology,* Vol. 128, No. 5, pp. 245-324. Cambridge, Mass.

Stuart, L.C.
    1958   A study of the herpetofauna of the Uaxactun-Tikal area of northern El Petén, Guatemala. *Contribution from the Laboratory of Vertebrate Biology, University of Michigan,* No. 75. Ann Arbor.

Tozzer, A. M.
    1911   Preliminary study of the ruins of Tikal, Guatemala. *Memoirs, Peabody Museum, Harvard University,* Vol. 5, no. 2. Cambridge, Mass.

Walker, L. C., Jr.
    1959   Maya graffiti as art. *Art in the South, Southwestern Louisiana Institute,* pp. 193-200. Lafayette.

Scene incised upon bone from Burial 116, Temple I.

ACKNOWLEDGMENTS

The excavations and study of Tikal have been carried out over the years since 1956 by a group of archaeologists, architects, surveyors, laboratory technicians and other specialists, numbering over one hundred, and coming from the United States, Guatemala, Canada, Mexico, Switzerland, and Germany. The scientific and, here, hopefully the popular success of Tikal is of their making, supported by the extraordinary contributions of foundations, private individuals, and government, as well as the steady labors of a work force that counted in it men who came to know what it meant to do their job matchlessly. In the writing of this guide, the author is obliged particularly to Viviam Broman Morales, Christopher Jones, Peter D. Harrison, and Dennis E. Puleston.

Linton Satterthwaite is to be thanked for his valuable suggestions during the writing of the Appendix devoted to the Maya calendar; if faults remain in this brief treatment of a most difficult subject, they are the author's responsibility. Should dedications be in order in this, a guide book, those that have devoted these long years to Tikal would wish to honor Linton Satterthwaite for his constructive guidance in what turned out to be an undertaking of proportions barely perceptible at its outset.

The burden of editing was carried by Geraldine Bruckner and Louis de V. Day, Jr. I also wish to thank my wife, Ann, for often keeping me from the pitfalls of extraneous detail that would confuse rather than enlighten the visitor to Tikal. All illustrations are by the author with the following exceptions: pp. 7, 19, 22, 24, 63, 89, 93, 102 lower right, cover and back cover, Jaime Freire; p. 5, Louis de V. Day, Jr.; p. 8, Diego Molina; pp. 9, 17, 52, 102, 104 upper, 106, Virginia Greene; pp. 10, 14, George Holton; pp 11, 105 upper, Fern Stanford; p. 12, Moeshlin and Bauer, Basle; p. 13 right, Eusebio Lara; p. 15, Alfred Percival Maudslay (with permission of the Brithis Museum); p. 20, Carr and Hazard, Tikal Report No. 11; pp. 26, 67, H. Stanley Loten; p. 81, Wilbur Pearson; p.84, Antonio Tejeda F.; p.85, Norman Johnson; p. 91, (map) Tikal National Project; p. 96 National Museum of Archaeology and Ethnology; p. 108, Dennis E. Puleston and Donald W. Calleder, Jr.; p. 113, Mona Heath; p. 117, Helen Trik; p. 118, Aubrey S. Trik; pp. 125, 128, Andy Seuffert.

-WILLIAM R. COE

Philadelphia
June, 1967

Drawing of bound captive,
4 ¹/₂ inches high,
incised on a bone
discovered in Burial 116.

The Author:

William R. Coe has been associated with the Tikal project of the University Museum, the University of Pennsylvania since 1956. He was Field Director from 1962 until 1969 when the University Museum turned the Project over to the Guatemalan government. He had previously done field work in Yucatán, Belice, El Salvador and Belice. He obtained his Ph. D. in Anthropology from the University of Pennsylvania in 1958. At present he is working full time in the publication of the Tikal Reports.

1st.   Edition, 1967
2nd.   Printing, June 1969
3rd.   Printing, May 1970
4th.   Printing, June 1973
5th.   and 6th. Printing, 1974
7th.   Printing, May 1975
8th.   Printing, April 1976
9th.   Printing, October 1977
10th.   Printing, October 1978
11th.   Printing, April 1980
12th.   Printing, July 1985
13th,   Printing, October 1986
14th.   Printing, March 1988
2nd.   Edition, June 1988
2nd.   Printing, February 1990
3rd.   Printing, October 1990
4th.   Printing, July 1992
5th.   Printing, April 1993
6th.   Printing, April 1994